DANIEL FAST JOURNEY

DANIEL FAST JOURNEY

A FASTING BREAKTHROUGH FOR PHYSICAL HEALTH, MENTAL CLARITY, AND SPIRITUAL GROWTH

STEPHANIE C. HODGES

Unless otherwise noted, scripture quotations marked NASB are taken from the New American Standard NASB® Copyright © 1960, 1971, 1977,1995, 2020 by The Lockman Foundation. A Corporation Not for Profit. La Habra, CA. All rights reserved. Used by permission.

Scripture quotations marked NKJV are taken from the New King James Version NKJV Copyright © 1982 by Thomas Nelson, Inc. All rights reserved. Used by permission.

ISBN: 978-1-7362179-0-0 (electronic)
ISBN: 978-1-7362179-2-4 (paperback)

DISCLAIMER
This book, Daniel Fast Journey, contains information about health, wellness, and nutrition for educational purposes only. This book is not written by a medical professional and is not intended to be a substitute for medical advice. Consult your physician or a health care professional before making any changes to your diet or fitness program.

To Brian
Thank you for supporting this book from the very beginning. And for being the world's best husband, father, and friend.

Contents

Introduction

Have you ever felt like you were in the movie *Groundhog Day?* In this comedy released in 1993, the plot centers on a character who gets stuck in time. Every morning when his alarm goes off, it's February second, again and again. He's forced to repeat the same day until he finally breaks the cycle.

Our daily grind can sometimes feel that same way, like we're stuck on repeat. Get up, eat, rush to the car, check e-mail, pick up kids, drop into bed . . . days can be full of activity but empty of purpose. Like we're constantly running but never getting anywhere.

If you feel like a hamster in a wheel, you're not alone. We aren't meant to be going and doing all the time. Our bodies need rest, our souls need quiet space, and our spirits need refreshing. We aren't guaranteed we'll ever find spare time, so we have to intentionally make time to stop, connect to God, and align with our purpose.

The *Daniel Fast Journey* is about creating those moments of pause in our lives. Fasting is an ancient practice that is more relevant today than ever before from a spiritual, mental, and physical health standpoint. This is especially true given the pace of our lives and the low-nutritional quality of the standard western diet. Maybe you've heard this statement: you are a spiritual being, you have a soul, and you live in a physical body. Fasting is a practice that touches every element of the spirit, soul, and body.

The Daniel Fast isn't a twenty-one day health plan or a one-time transformation. Fasting is a spiritual practice that can be incorporated into your life at regular intervals for years to come. Just like prayer and reading the Bible, fasting has been a key part of Christian living throughout church history.

Serving as a vital checkpoint, fasting is an opportunity to clear the clutter, noise, and junk from your system. In turn, as you lean into God and listen for His direction, you will become spiritually full, mentally well, and physically energized. James 4:8 assures us of this: "Draw near to God and He will draw near to you."

You may desire to draw nearer to God and to nourish your body and soul, but you aren't sure if fasting is for you. I write about the Daniel Fast with the hope of making fasting accessible to everyone. Most people do not fast at all, sometimes because fasting seems like an extreme practice, and they feel unequipped to take on that challenge. However, the Daniel Fast is a great first step into fasting as a spiritual and health discipline and can be done even during a busy season or with other health considerations.

Before we dive into all that fasting means for you, I want to briefly share why I chose the Daniel Fast and how this book came to be. This story is a reminder that answers don't always arrive immediately, but sometimes the long, slow journey is ultimately the best way to travel.

Why I Chose the Daniel Fast

When I hear the word *journey*, I picture someone with a backpack at the base of a dirt road that leads to distant hills. The sun is rising, the air is cool, and the only noise is a bird chirping. This picturesque and peaceful vision is the journey I would like to go on.

But when I wake up in the morning, the landscape in front of me is the opposite. It's messy, loud, and fast-paced. There are kids to get ready, e-mails to check, and forever more projects to tackle. Finding time to invest in my health and take needed breaks is never easy, but always necessary.

While health has always been a huge priority in my life, I was about to discover just how big a challenge it could be to find time for fitness and wellness in my late twenties when I became pregnant with my first of three children. I have two sons and a daughter, all about two years apart in age, which means I was pregnant or nursing for about six years straight.

Pregnancy, infant, and toddler years all have their unique challenges. When your children are young and completely dependent on you, your world revolves to a degree around protecting and caring for them. That reality can affect if and how you fast. When my children were little, I needed steady energy in order to survive physically, mentally, and emotionally. So during those times, any practice of fasting had to be the Daniel Fast.

Many of you may be in a similar circumstance. You might be a mom with young kids or have physical limitations for fasting. It could also be that you have a demanding job or another unique scenario. And if you have never fasted before or have limited experience, it can be an extreme shock to your body to go into a full fast. These are all reasons it makes sense to try a Daniel Fast, with guidance from your doctor.

Where Did This Book Come From?

In 2010, I discovered something called blogging. Bear with me because it was a profound revelation at that time—especially for a nerdy girl who loved researching, reading, and writing. The realization that anyone (even I) could easily hit publish and reach people with a helpful message was exhilarating—even if my two biggest fans were my mom and my sister.

When I started blogging, it was a hobby where I could share advice to help others get fit and stay healthy. At the time, I was working full-time at a corporate gym as a group fitness instructor and personal trainer along with maintaining the facility and presenting wellness seminars.

I was (and still am) passionate about everything related to wellness. I assumed my entire career would be in the fitness industry, and blogging was just a hobby on the side. I dabbled over the years with half a dozen different blog iterations, including a family photo blog after my first son was born. When my second son was born twenty-two months later, all activities non-essential to survival were put on the back burner.

No more teaching fitness classes, no more part-time virtual assistant work, and definitely no more blogging. Since I didn't even have time to shower, I didn't have time to put hundreds of words together into a coherent blog post. I decided to not work outside the home and completely focus on my baby and toddler during this season.

I was praying one morning when my second son was about a year old. God gave me a very specific verse and directive to start blogging again, so I began from scratch. The blog was centered around healthy living topics targeted to moms with young kids, as a reflection of my own life and experience at the time.

The following January, I posted the meal plan, shopping list, and recipes I had organized for my personal Daniel Fast. Little did I know that the topic would become the most popular of anything I had written on the blog. Ever.

I was grateful that I'd provided content that people found useful in the sea of information on the Internet. I was also shocked by some criticism I received, which I'll tell you more about later in the book. The negative feedback was minimal, but those attacks and doubts caused me to pause, dive into the Bible, and do some research to ensure I was clear about what I believed regarding fasting and how a Daniel Fast compared to a more traditional water-only complete fast (and I strongly encourage you to do the same).

Meanwhile, everyone else was leaning in and asking for additional resources such as:

When are you going to post meal plans for weeks three and four?

Do you have all this information in one document?

Is there a book?

As much as I wanted to add Daniel Fast resources and put everything into a book, the timing wasn't right. I was pregnant with our third child and had gone back to work. Although I had no time to write, thoughts of the blog and writing the Daniel Fast book were always in the back of my mind.

Four years later, I was enjoying a summer beach vacation with my family. One early morning, as I sat on the balcony listening to the waves, the Lord instructed me to do three things: go to a women's retreat happening that September, write a free devotional to put on the blog, and write the Daniel Fast book.

However, just because the Lord calls you to do something doesn't mean it'll be easy! You are now reading the book I was called to write that summer of 2019, but only after several stops and restarts, challenges and setbacks, and working through a 2020 COVID pandemic that turned everyone's life upside down. Our personal comfort and ease cannot always be the measure for ensuring that we're living according to God's purpose. He is so faithful to sustain us, protect us, and provide for us in what He has called us to do—there is peace in the boat even when the storm is raging all around.

To close the loop on this story, in case you're wondering, I did go to the retreat that September, and it was a life-changing experience. And a free devotional can be found at danielfastjourney.com along with recipes and other resources to supplement this book.

Live for More

I share this personal story for two reasons: to give you some background on how this book came to exist and because you can apply the takeaways to many situations, including fasting. Reaching your goals and finding answers to your questions is a path that sometimes has unexpected turns and breaks along the way; it's not always smooth and straight from start to finish.

Dreams take time. We assume we'll get a quick fix and instant result—especially in a culture of microwaves, WiFi, and instant feedback. But the Bible uses metaphors of agriculture, not industry. We can't always produce the results we want on our timeline; sometimes we have to plant seeds, water them, and wait for the process of growth so they can mature and bear fruit. The process is time-consuming and less predictable than following a set of cookie-cutter instructions.

Know your season. You can't say yes to everything all the time. Good ideas abound, but you are the only one who knows what your priorities are and what your schedule can handle. You may have a

God-given dream, but right now may not be the ideal time to start on it. Wait and listen for confirmation from the Lord about timing.

Be obedient. You have to be obedient both to say no—and also to say yes. If the Lord has convicted you about something that needs to change, He will supply you with everything you need, including time, finances, people, and resources. But only you can take the action steps necessary to move forward.

You can't eliminate every challenge and plan every detail in advance, but if through this fasting experience, God asks you to realign your priorities, or to let some things go and start doing others, then your response can be a confident yes. Fasting won't be easy. That's part of the process. When things don't feel fun and comfortable, it's not a sign to quit but to press in, rely on God, and keep going. As you remember the reasons you decided to fast, you can confidently pray and persevere.

Jesus fasted. Moses and Daniel fasted. Many other heroes of the faith also fasted. Rest assured that you are journeying on a well-traveled path that will lead you to greater intimacy with God. Get ready to refresh your spirit, renew your mind, and revitalize your body.

What to Expect in this Book

You may be excited to get to the meal plan and recipes. But before diving into what to eat, there's an important foundation for fasting. To repeat an earlier point, this book isn't just a diet with a twenty-one day meal plan. It's about fasting as a practice to realign your spirit, soul, and body. With this goal in mind, it's important to examine each of these facets before you begin. Fasting will be challenging. When those difficult moments arise, you want to be sure of why you've committed to fasting.

Part one of this book is about the purpose behind fasting. Chapter one lays a foundation and purpose for fasting, and chapter two looks at holistic health. You'll see how fasting impacts your spirit and soul and how a plant-based diet benefits your body. In part two, we'll look at the spiritual basis for fasting. Whether you're doing a partial fast or complete fast, the biblical precedent and motivations for fasting are important. Chapter four will specifically look at the lives of Daniel and Jesus and how they fasted. Part three covers essential preparation. As you take away physical food, you need to be prepared to nourish yourself with soul food. Chapter five covers spiritual disciplines to consider during your time of fasting. Chapter six will help you physically and logistically prepare for fasting.

Part four is the discussion of what to eat. This also includes important meal preparation and planning tips. Finally, part five contains the twenty-one day meal plan and recipe guide.

Every chapter will close with a "Your Journey" section. This will allow you some space for reflection and application. Also, remember to go to danielfastjourney.com/bookresources to get the bonus fasting journal sheet, printable twenty-one-day meal plan, and other resources.

Fasting is not the latest fad, it's actually a well-established practice that has been around for thousands of years, so it's time for us to sit up and take note. "Thus says the Lord, 'Stand by the ways and see and ask for the ancient paths, where the good way is, and walk in it; and you will find rest for your souls'." (Jer 6:16) Time to say a prayer and dive in!

PART ONE
WHY FASTING MATTERS

Chapter 1

Where Are You Going? Why Fasting Matters

But Daniel made up his mind that he would not defile himself with the king's choice food or with the wine which he drank; so he sought permission from the commander of the officials that he might not defile himself. —Dan 1:8

Ultimately we fast simply because we want God more than we want anything this world has to offer us. —John Piper

The book of Daniel tells the story of a young Jewish man taken into captivity under the Neo-Babylonian Empire. He was removed from his home and brought into the king's court to be trained in a foreign language, literature, and customs. For the seventy years he was in captivity, Daniel rose up and stood out because of his excellent spirit. Although he adapted to his new environment, he remained fiercely uncompromised when it came to matters of faith.

Daniel had to deal with political maneuverings and death threats. But throughout his life, the Lord always guided, protected, and delivered him from any harm. This gave him the boldness needed to not just survive but to thrive no matter what difficulties came his way.

Through it all, he realized small details are a big deal and was diligent about his daily practices. He was clear about drawing lines. There were certain actions he wouldn't take and other habits he was staunchly committed to continuing no matter the repercussions. He refused to eat food that would defile him. He also prayed faithfully, three times a day, even when the consequence was to be thrown into the lions' den.

Daniel was under immense pressure to fit in, compromise, and cater to cultural expectations—maybe you can relate. But Daniel remained undefiled and uncompromising, always putting God first and living an inspiring life of integrity. Right now, the buzzword is *authenticity*, which holds the same ideal as integrity: that there is unity in our inner and outer worlds. We long to be confident in who we are and what we believe, not swayed by our current situation or surrounding environment but consistent at all times.

If we want this level of integrity and confidence, we first have to examine what we believe and who we rely on. Fasting is one of the best practices to help us silence the noise, hear from God, and determine the truth. The next step is to build the internal strength and conviction to consistently walk out a faith-filled life that is centered on God first. Fasting strengthens us spiritually to do just that.

When we have Daniel's level of integrity, the routine details of our lives will align with our big-picture values. We won't have the unsettled feeling of trying to navigate two different lives, with the way we start Sunday morning feeling a world away from how we end Friday evening.

From the king's palace to his private prayer room, Daniel held the same standard, and our ability to do the same starts with asking the right questions and establishing the right habits. Do you involve God in the day-to-day details? Are you making decisions that align with His will? Are you pursuing health in all areas? How often do you hear God's direction, and how often are you asking for it?

Our modern world is loud and fast-paced. It's hard to hear the still, small voice of the Lord when we're constantly bombarded with opinions, advice, and marketing. These messages would lead us to believe that everything about our lives can be fixed or improved with ten steps or the right product in hand.

As we consume more, do more, and commit to more, we can end up feeling depleted because we're chasing the wrong things. Possessions, promotions, and popularity can never truly satisfy us. Although the next *thing* we're chasing is supposed to be the missing link to a peaceful and joy-filled life, we end up exhausted and drained, not fulfilled as we had hoped.

Chronic busyness negatively affects our physical, mental, and spiritual health. Research overwhelmingly suggests that the majority of the population suffers to some degree from being anxious, unhealthy, and fatigued. Our bodies need sufficient sleep, quality nutrition, and daily physical movement. These routines require a time investment; shortcuts won't cut it long-term.

Perhaps the answer is not to move faster and do more but to slow down and do less. This is where fasting comes in. The ancient practice of fasting helps us strip away the excess and create stillness and space. As we'll examine later in this book, fasting was a key spiritual practice throughout the Old and New Testaments.

The Hebrew word for fast is *tsuwm*, meaning to "cover the mouth." The primary idea is that the mouth is shut[1]. A closed mouth isn't eating and also isn't talking. From a physical standpoint, when we fast and consume less, then our bodies have time for complete digestion, to thoroughly process and expel some of the preservatives and excess that have built up in our systems.

Fasting isn't just about removing food, it's about feeding our spirits and souls in a way that truly nourishes and sustains us. Rather than constantly consuming, we take time to stop, cover our mouth, and listen to God. We acknowledge that we don't have every answer and can't do it all ourselves; we need Him.

Fasting is a time to seek God, meditate on His truth, and reflect on our lives. And in that process is the opportunity to clear out toxic patterns, renew our minds, and strengthen our spirits.

The idea of a complete, water-only fast can be intimidating for many people. In fact, it can be so overwhelming that many won't try fasting because there is never a "right time," or they dread the process.

Complete fasting may not be safe for others because of health conditions, medications, pregnancy, or nursing.

Maybe you've never fasted before. Perhaps you've tried to fast, and it didn't end well. Or maybe you're ready to make fasting a more regular practice in your life. If any of these scenarios resonate, then the Daniel Fast is an accessible step and safe way to cultivate a regular habit of fasting and an overall healthier lifestyle for years to come.

What is the Daniel Fast?

A Daniel Fast, based on the first chapter of the book of Daniel, is a partial fast in which you eat only plant-based foods and drink only water. A Daniel Fast plan could easily be confused with a diet. Although spiritual fasts and the biblical basis for fasting are not primarily motivated by a desire for physical benefits, fasting ultimately affects the health of your entire being.

You could read through the first two parts of this book and take away notes for a spiritual fast. Or you could pull out parts four and five and view it primarily as a healthy eating plan centered on plant-based foods. But my hope is that you will see how the Daniel Fast unites and impacts both spiritual and physical health. Our spirit, soul, and body are so complexly intertwined that it's nearly impossible to treat them in an isolated fashion. Although the fast we're discussing in this book originates from a spiritual purpose and desire to worship God and be obedient to what He has called us to do, the effects of fasting are far-reaching.

Our bodies were created by God, and we're charged to take care of our physical health. John said, "I pray that in all respects you may prosper and be in good health, just as your soul prospers." (3 John 2) In Romans 12:1 Paul urges us, "By the mercies of God, to present your bodies a living and holy sacrifice, acceptable to God, which is your spiritual service of worship." Maintaining our health helps us stay fit to serve God in whatever He calls us to do.

As a partial fast, you may limit the amount you eat or windows of time when you eat on a Daniel Fast, but the primary focus is on restricting certain types of foods. On a Daniel Fast, you'll abstain from all animal products, alcohol, processed snacks, and baked goods.

Considering the average American diet, this is a significant shift for most people. A Daniel Fast is not necessarily an "easier" way to fast. You will still be challenged with cravings and hunger, based on the limited options available.

Although you may experience some initial side effects, it's beneficial for your body to remove excess sugar, salt, and preservatives; the end results will far outweigh the momentary discomfort. The wholesome plant-based foods you consume on a Daniel Fast will replace the processed fillers and additives with natural fiber, vitamins, and minerals. By the end, you'll be experiencing better health and increased energy.

The Daniel Fast has grown in popularity in recent history. When fasting is mentioned in the Bible, it's typically in reference to not eating at all. But there are also biblical examples of people modifying certain aspects of their diet, which is where the concept of a partial fast originated.

The eating guidelines for the Daniel Fast come from a story at the beginning of the book of Daniel. This ten-day period is actually called a test, not a fast. His main motivation was to avoid any degradation from food and wine that may have been sacrificed to idols or not prepared according to Jewish law:

But Daniel resolved not to defile himself with the royal food and wine, and he asked the chief official for permission not to defile himself this way . . . 'Please test your servants for ten days: Give us nothing but vegetables to eat and water to drink.'

(Dan 1:8,12)

There are two other instances of Daniel fasting that are recorded in the Bible. In Daniel 9:3, Daniel turned to the Lord with prayer and petition, in fasting and sackcloth. Daniel also referred to a period where he mourned for three weeks and ate no choice food, meat, or wine, and used no lotions (Dan 10:3). We'll discuss these fasts again in chapter four of this book.

Based on these passages, the standard length of a Daniel Fast is usually ten days or twenty-one days. However, there's no rule about how long your fast must be—that's something to pray about and decide individually.

Thayer's Greek Lexicon defines fasting as "abstain[ing] as a religious exercise from food and drink: either entirely, if the fast lasted but a single day, or from customary food and choice nourishment, if continued for several days."[II] Some would claim that a true biblical fast involves abstaining from all food. Yet we can see from this reference and Daniel's example that longer fasts may be partial fasts, abstaining from specific types of foods and luxuries.

Because Daniel's daily menu isn't specifically spelled out in the Bible, exactly what foods can be consumed on the Daniel Fast has been open to interpretation. The main point of clarity provided by the Bible is to not consume meat or alcohol.

A modern Daniel Fast meal plan typically abstains from all animal products and processed foods and includes only grains, vegetables, fruits, beans, legumes seeds, and anything that comes directly from the ground. We'll be discussing more details on how to make those decisions about what to eat on your fast in Part Four of this book.

When we fast, our focus is not primarily on food but on drawing closer to God and growing more sensitive in our spirits. As we decidedly turn away from the world and towards God, we can better hear His voice, clarify our priorities, and renew our energy.

It's important to note that fasting isn't recommended for anyone who has struggled or is currently struggling with eating disorders. Eating habits can also be connected to painful memories and trauma. If you think this may be the case for you, be sure to surround yourself with professional help and a strong support system before any attempt to fast.

The Countercultural Slow Journey

The word "journey" is defined as traveling from one place to another, usually taking a rather long time. It's a passage or progress from one stage to another.[III] We all have a life journey, but whether we purposefully progress is up to us. We are responsible for the route we choose and how we travel.

Books and blogs are filled with techniques on how to be more efficient and productive, but where do you find the tools to increase patience, cultivate endurance, and purposely move slowly with intention? The very nature of a journey is that it takes a *long time*. The goal is to continue walking in your purpose as long as you're breathing, which requires pacing for the long haul. Instead of rushing to reach the next milestone, we can learn to embrace the process and find the right pace that propels us forward without burning us out.

Every parent of adult children has told me that time goes by more quickly than you think and that you'll blink, and your kids will be grown. That can be challenging to imagine as a young parent when you're in the midst of sleepless nights and smelly diapers. The days feel quite long when you're up for twenty hours out of twenty-four. But whether you have young children or not, you can't ignore the reality that times pass, seasons change, and if we aren't mindful and appreciative, we can end up breezing past critical moments.

We may have great intentions but unknowingly veer off track. We can meander onto the wrong path because we're distracted. Or we may be stuck in patterns that cause us to go in circles. And we can also be frantic in our activity, but not making forward progress.

Right now is the perfect time to pull out your metaphorical compass and get your bearings. Check in on the state of your health, your schedule, and your priorities:

- Do you know where you're going and why?
- Are you healthy in every aspect of your life (spiritually, mentally, physically)?
- Are you traveling at the right pace and getting enough rest?
- Are you surrounded by the right people, resources, and environment?
- Are you including God in your planning process?

For too many of us, the answers to these questions don't paint an ideal picture. We are rushing, multitasking, and moving on autopilot. We're looking for a quick fix, and chasing the latest popular diet fad. We are so consumed with tasks to check off of our lists that we forget to check in with people—or with God.

We need balance, which is not the ability to do everything perfectly and equally, but the ability to prioritize the right things. When life feels out of balance, it's because immediate, urgent tasks are dominating our time and pushing aside our long-term, important priorities. And when you're off balance, you're more likely to fall and hurt yourself.

Jesus regularly made it a priority to spend time alone with His Father, sometimes entire nights in prayer. He also spent forty days fasting before He entered public ministry. He taught His disciples about when and how they would fast when He was gone, which we'll discuss more in chapter four.

When we fast, we're shutting off temporary solutions and momentary satisfaction to instead pursue the deep joy and peace that can only be found in Christ. When you have a major decision to make, do you push for an answer as quickly as possible, or would you consider taking forty days (or more) to pray and wait to hear from the Lord before making any moves?

While we desire to put Christ first in our lives, pursuing discipline, endurance, and long-suffering isn't necessarily fun; however, it is essential to living a kingdom life. The Bible offers counterintuitive principles such as the first will be last and the greatest among you is a servant.

These standards conflict with what the world tells us, both overtly and subtly, but are the keys to success. Our fast-paced, technology-filled culture drives us to habits that negatively affect our health and cause many of us to feel lethargic, battle chronic pain, and endure physical discomfort. These serious physical issues can hinder not only our longevity but also our present quality of life. If we don't properly care for our bodies, our ability to walk out our purpose will be hindered by poor health.

We've heard great tips about how to be healthier and get fit. There are simple practices like taking the stairs or parking farther away so you can walk, but it's easy to ignore this advice. It's more convenient to park by the store entrance because we're usually in a hurry. In fact, we can now save even more time with curbside pickup—we don't even have to stand up, much less walk.

Technology can be a help and a hindrance. While some tasks are more efficient with an app, technology ultimately adds to our total workload. Messages and notifications constantly flash on the screen, demanding to be checked. Social media mimics connection and social activity but often falls short of authentic relationships and support. And this is all available twenty-four hours a day with no off-hours or quiet time.

We can also cut corners when it comes to nurturing our spiritual health. Our busy pace can drive us towards a spiritual life that is shallow and disengaged. We may substitute quick inspiration and motivation for taking the time for meditation, study, and developing a deep level of intimacy with God.

Picture what a healthy marriage looks like for a minute and how you would describe it. How strong will the relationship be if the couple only interacts on a group date a few times a month? Or if conversations only happen while driving in the car or doing dishes in the kitchen?

For some of us, this is what our relationship with God looks like: it starts and ends with going to church on Sunday. Maybe we listen to a podcast in the car or tag our praying and devotional time onto other activities like chores or working out. But to develop an intimate relationship, there's no substitute for quality time and undivided attention. This is true for relationships with others and with God.

Our relationship with God needs to be cultivated, and as we look to biblical examples, we need to consider what their lifestyle looked like compared to our own. Modern conveniences such as quick modes of transportation didn't exist. There were no jets, bullet trains, or speed boats. They had to journey through the wilderness or walk a full day to the next town. Although walking required more time, there were benefits to the slow-paced journey.

Consider Jesus and His disciples. As they traveled together, they had ample time for deep conversations that presented new perspectives and shifted paradigms. They shared personal moments. They noticed fig trees by the road. They had time to ask questions.

Along the journey, the disciples were able to see Christ's love in real time. They observed His response to a blind man, a tax collector in a tree, and a woman who had been bleeding for twelve years. When people interrupted Jesus, He wasn't too busy to stop, look them in the eye, and address their concerns.

The Lord invites us to walk with Him, but we have to make the decision to slow down. We're worried about not having time to complete everything on our list, but we should be more afraid of missing quality moments and the more important life lessons because we're in too much of a hurry. It's hard to go slow in a fast-paced world, but fasting is an opportunity to do just that.

Your Journey

What have your previous experiences with fasting been like? Or if you've never fasted, what is your impression of fasting? As you prepare to fast, you'll want to record your thoughts, revelations, and prayers. You can use any notebook, record your thoughts electronically, or print the "Planning & Reflection Journal" and "Daily Journal" from danielfastjourney.com/bookresources.

Chapter 1 Reflections

• Have you had prior experience fasting? If so, what were the high and low points?

• Why do you feel the Daniel Fast would be a good fit for you (or why not)?

• On a scale of 1–10, how would you rate your current state of health in the following areas: spirit, soul, and body? Why did you give yourself those scores?

Chapter 2

How Will You Get There? A Spirit, Soul, Body Journey

*Jesus answered, "The foremost is, 'Hear, O Israel! The Lord our God is one Lord;
and you shall love the Lord your God with all your heart, and with all your soul, and
with all your mind, and with all your strength." —Mark 12:29–30*

*Fasting helps to express, to deepen, and to confirm the resolution that we are
ready to sacrifice anything, to sacrifice ourselves, to attain what we seek for the kingdom of God . . . Prayer is the reaching out after God and the unseen; fasting the letting go of all that is of the seen and temporal. —Andrew Murray*

So why have you decided to pick up a book about the Daniel Fast?
Maybe you've participated in a Daniel Fast in the past and you're
looking for some new recipes, or maybe you've heard about fasting
and have some hopes that it will benefit your spiritual life or physical
health. Whatever your primary motivation for a Daniel Fast may be,

fasting will inevitably affect your spirit, soul, and body, sometimes in unexpected ways.

This chapter starts with a verse in which Jesus states the greatest commandment, which is loving God with all of our heart, soul, mind, and strength—every single part of our being. The concept of *holistic health* reflects a similar thought. A holistic approach to science or health emphasizes the whole over individual parts and looks for connections rather than treating individual symptoms in isolation.[IV]

It's important to consider how fasting impacts us as a holistic being. It may feel more holy to say we're fasting purely for spiritual reasons and don't care about the physical. But because God created the world and everything in it, including our bodies, no topic is off-limits. He doesn't necessarily delineate and define things the way we do. As we fast, we can gain a new perspective on what it means to love Him with all our heart, soul, mind, and strength.

Spirit, Soul, and Body

From an overall health standpoint, it can be difficult to separate the interrelated causes and effects impacting our mind and body. It's rare to find one simple cause and one direct solution that will lead you to a state of perfect health. We're complicated beings. So when we treat only part of the problem, we'll only get a partial solution.

Consider the following scenario: You're experiencing pain and cannot sleep well. After a night of tossing and turning, you get out of bed late. Not only are you rushed and behind schedule, but you've also missed your morning quiet time with the Lord.

Now you're physically tired, still in pain, mentally stressed, and emotionally cranky. You may try to attack this situation by praying harder or commanding yourself to think positive thoughts. As you struggle through the day, you may blame the devil, your faulty alarm clock, or yourself for lack of self-control and willpower.

There's a spiritual element to every situation, which requires prayer, but what about the first domino that caused this cascade of events? Your body is in pain, which is a signal that something is wrong. Instead of ignoring it, if you investigate and resolve the physical pain, you can get the proper sleep you need, which impacts the other pieces of this chain reaction.

You also can't ignore the more urgent signals your body may be trying to send you. Pain can be a sign of a more serious physical problem that needs a doctor's investigation, or it can be a cry for emotional help. Sometimes physical pain is your body's way of signaling you about stress or underlying issues that need to be dealt with.

You've probably heard expressions like, "I have a knot in my stomach" or "I feel like I have the weight of the world on my shoulders." Many similar sayings reflect the fact that our mental and emotional well-being are intricately tied to our physical health. Because this is true, you can direct your thoughts and emotions for good. Prayer, quiet moments of deep breathing, and social support all help you survive and thrive throughout your day, whatever else may be going on.

Paul referenced all elements of our being in his letter to the Thessalonians. He encouraged the members of the church: "Now may the God of peace Himself sanctify you entirely; and may your spirit and soul and body be preserved complete, without blame at the coming of our Lord Jesus Christ." (1Thes 5:23) The goal is for every part to be healthy and unified, and in this verse we see a clear distinction of our spirit, soul, and body as three entities.

The word spirit comes from the Greek word *pneuma* which is the vital principle animating the body and is also the word used for the Holy Spirit. Soul is *psyche*, which includes the seat of feelings, desires, affections, and aversions. The body is *soma* which is used both literally to mean the body of people or animals, or figuratively as a united group of people.[v] We have these three parts—body, soul, and spirit—to steward and care for.

In the story of creation, God said, "Let us make man in our image." (Gen 1:26) He took man from the dust of the earth and breathed life into him. When Jesus came, He explained that after being born in the flesh, you have to be born again of the Spirit to enter the kingdom of God (John 3:5–6). Once we're born again, we're a new creation. Our spirit is alive in Christ but still housed in a physical body.

Jesus instructed His followers to pray for God's kingdom to come, and for His will to be done on earth as it is in heaven (Matt 6:10). As spiritual beings in a physical world, it can be difficult to maintain this heavenly perspective when our days seem to be consumed with worldly obligations. How can you bring eternal purpose into daily mundane tasks?

Fasting is one way to break down the barriers and put a spiritual lens on everyday activities. On an average day, even after committing to focus on God, we can easily get distracted. But when we fast, our growling stomachs are a constant reminder of who needs to be first in our lives and serve as a mental checkpoint. When we fast, we're depending on God for everything, denying our flesh, and focusing on our spirit.

In Galatians 5:16 Paul says to walk by the Spirit so you will not carry out the desires of the flesh, because the flesh and Spirit are in opposition to each other. Which will you choose to side with? You can read the list of deeds of the flesh and fruits of the spirit in Galatians 5:19–23.

With that said, it's important in this process that we don't start to designate everything related to our body and the physical world as bad or inferior. Our physical body can be described as flesh, which has practical desires for hunger, thirst, and sleep, but our bodies are not inherently evil. As the scripture says, it's the *lusts (or desires)* of the flesh that can lead us astray (1 John 2:16).

Here is where the soul plays a key role. The soul is commonly defined as the mind, will, and emotions. With the free will we've been given, it's our responsibility to choose wisely. This applies to the thoughts we entertain and the emotions we dwell on. In the Psalms, David repeatedly talks to his soul, providing encouragement and reminding himself to praise God and meditate on His goodness. We need to focus on soul care daily, especially when we fast, and chapter five discusses spiritual disciplines that provide the right spiritual nourishment for our souls.

Fasting can expose where our cravings originate, and the reasons why we eat. Too often, we don't reach for food because we're hungry and need physical fuel but rather to numb our feelings, cope with stress, or distract ourselves from boredom.

When our temporary food fix is unavailable, we have to confront our thoughts, feelings, and triggers. We can't ignore and stuff issues; we have to work through them. Without comfort food to distract us, God is ready and waiting for the opportunity to meet all our needs, whether that be through others or through His wisdom.

Everyone needs support through prayer and godly counsel. Just as we can't separate our spirit from our body, we can't separate ourselves as individuals from the body of the church. Having mentors and spiritual leaders in our lives is key. If fasting is new for you, it's wise to have someone who can offer advice based on their experience.

We could spend a lifetime studying the nuances of spirit, soul, and body. This is a very brief summary of a huge subject and we have only scratched the surface. As you begin fasting, you can rest assured that your health will benefit in every dimension. Next, we're going to specifically look at the positive physical effects of the Daniel Fast eating plan.

Eat to Live

We are created by God, and our bodies are the temple of the Holy Spirit. There's a difference between being concerned about how our bodies look (usually influenced by cultural standards and comparing ourselves to others) and caring about how our bodies function.

When we honor our bodies and take care of our physical health, we are stewarding what God has created and blessed us with. These bodies are the vessels we have to carry us through our lifetime, and our health directly affects our ability to run with purpose, fulfill our calling, and make an impact on the world around us. It's about much more than appearance.

One of the most significant factors impacting our health is how we eat. Opinions and advice on the optimal diet are plentiful and often conflict with each other. Over the past forty years, we've been told to eat as little fat as possible, that we can eat a high-fat diet but not carbohydrates, and that some fat is okay but we have to eat the right kind.

And if that isn't confusing enough, the food labels are also misleading. Food labels claim to be healthy because their product is organic, gluten-free, or has protein. There is a deeply entrenched idea that we need lots of protein to lose weight and feel full. Yes, adequate protein is vital to health, but the majority of Americans are already consuming more than the minimum recommended amount of protein.[VI]

The Recommended Daily Allowance (RDA) for protein is 0.8 grams per kilogram bodyweight, which means someone who weighs

150 pounds needs about 54 grams of protein a day.[VII] We also have to remember that protein is not limited to meat and supplements. Plant-based foods also naturally contain protein. You just have to eat a variety of plant-based foods, including whole grains and five or more servings of fruits and vegetables daily, to ensure you get all the essential amino acids found in a single serving of meat.

In spite of the contradictions, experts can probably agree on one thing: we consume too many highly processed foods. These foods are typically full of sugar, salt, and preservatives. Our bodies quickly store the excess calories as fat, and the other artificial chemicals and preservatives linger in our systems with debatable long-term effects.

With the excess amounts we eat, it's difficult for our body to properly break down, utilize, and eliminate what we consume. Over 40 percent of adults in the US are obese, and more on top of that are overweight. Obesity is linked to a wide range of health issues including stroke, type 2 diabetes, cancer, mental illness, and all causes of mortality.[VIII]

The Standard American Diet is energy rich (i.e., high calorie) but nutrient poor, which is contributing to these increasing rates of obesity and disease. When reading nutrition labels, we need to look at more than the number of calories, fat, carbohydrates, and protein. Our bodies need vitamins, minerals, fiber, and phytochemicals to be truly healthy and thriving, and are best able to break down and absorb these components in their natural form. Artificial, processed foods are no substitute for whole, plant-based foods if we're looking for optimal health.

With the Daniel Fast, we radically change these poor habits. With this type of fast, you're free to eat a wide range of fruits, vegetables, whole grains, beans, legumes, nuts, and seeds. For further encouragement on why it's beneficial to participate in a Daniel Fast from a physical standpoint, here are three diet studies that show the positive effects of eating primarily plant-based diets.

The China Study

Extensive epidemiological research was done over a twenty-year period in sixty-five China counties in the 1970s and 1980s. Researchers gathered data on diet and measured mortality rates from cancer and other chronic diseases.

Some counties consumed a more traditional Chinese diet. This included primarily vegan foods and a limited intake of animal products and processed foods. Other counties had increased their consumption of western foods, which also included a noticeably increased intake of meat.

The study showed a correlation between the consumption of animal protein and cancer.[IX] Ongoing work by researchers such as Dr. Colin Campbell and Dr. Caldwell Esselstyn has continued to link animal products with increased rates of cancer and heart disease. In addition, they have shown that a whole-food, plant-based diet can slow and even reverse the effects of disease. These two doctors are featured in the Forks Over Knives documentary and have since created numerous resources to help people move to a plant-based diet and live healthier lives.[X]

The Blue Zones

The "Blue Zones" are five hot spots of longevity around the globe. Dan Buettner has been studying the lifestyles of people in these areas for years in partnership with the National Geographic Society. They've identified several key habits that contribute to the long-lived, high-quality lives of Blue Zone members.

Blue Zones are areas with the highest concentrations of centenarians (100 plus years old) along with the lowest rates of disease while aging. These five geographical locations are Ikaria, Greece; Okinawa, Japan; Sardinia, Italy; Loma Linda, California; and the Nicoya Peninsula, Costa Rica.

Diet is certainly a key contributor to longevity in these areas. Although specific foods vary from one region to the next based on what's locally available, there are nutritional similarities. Analysis of eating habits across all zones shows a diet that is on average 95 percent plant-based and 5 percent animal-based.

In addition to meat, other animal products and manufactured foods are limited. The research shows Blue Zone residents eat meat less than two times a week, fish two times a week max, eggs two to four times a week, and consume limited amounts of dairy (and dairy from cow's milk is uncommon in these regions). The Blue Zone diet is predominantly made up of beans, whole grains, vegetables, fruits, and nuts.

Cornerstone habits of people in these regions extend beyond what to eat. People eat to live and live their lives to the full. Members of Blue

Zone areas have strong relational and community ties, focus on family first, and create social circles. Meals are enjoyed sitting down with loved ones, not on the go.

Natural movement is a key part of their daily lifestyle. Rather than targeted exercise sessions, they're naturally active throughout the day. It's also been found that people in these regions maintain a unique life perspective, naturally downplaying stress and fostering a strong sense of purpose.

You may be curious about the one Blue Zone location found in the United States. Loma Linda, California has a Seventh-day Adventist community that is a longevity hot spot. These members prioritize honoring the Sabbath on Saturday as a day of rest. They maintain strong social ties and focus on health—many follow a vegetarian diet. According to the Adventist Health Study funded by the National Institute of Health, the Adventists who consistently followed the teachings on health, including a focus on a plant-based diet, lived an average of ten years longer than those who didn't.[XI]

The Longevity Diet

Dr. Valter Longo was born in Italy but moved to the United States as a teenager. He attended school and decided to devote his life to studying aging, specifically how to age the healthiest way possible. Part of his inspiration was his relationship with Salvatore Caruso, a neighbor of his grandparents in Italy who lived to be 110 and followed a specific diet and activity regimen throughout his life.

Longo has studied the effects of fasting and a plant-based diet on longevity and health conditions including cancer, diabetes, cardiovascular disease, Alzheimer's, and inflammatory and autoimmune diseases. Longo's research involved studying the effect of fasting on mice with cancer. These studies found fasting could slow and potentially reverse cancer growth.

He has drawn conclusions from his research in support of eating a predominantly plant-based diet. Longo also says that a sufficient amount of protein is 0.31 to 0.36 grams of protein per pound of body weight. This is about 50 grams of protein for a 150 pounds person (very close to the national RDA).

Based on the positive effect of fasting in these studies and additional research, Longo has developed a protocol for intermittent fasting. With proper medical supervision at every phase, it's possible that fasting can improve longevity and slow or reverse certain diseases.[XII]

Misguided Motivations for Fasting

With all of this information about the spiritual and physical benefits of fasting, hopefully you're fired up and ready to take off. But before you get too far down the road, you need to be aware of a couple of potential pitfalls. Let's shift back to discussing our mindset.

We can easily fall into three traps or detrimental mindsets: fasting as a means to make us more righteous, confusing fasting with dieting for weight loss, and quitting too soon.

First, we have to remember that fasting is not a tool to manipulate God to answer our prayers or to make us more righteous. We don't earn spiritual points or increase our holiness because we fast. We are already righteous, forgiven, and saved by grace and Jesus, not by our own works. God loves us completely and unconditionally.

We aren't the first generation to have misguided motivations for fasting. Jesus chastised the Pharisees because they made a public demonstration of what should have been a private practice.

Jesus also tells a story about a tax collector and Pharisee praying in the temple. The Pharisee thanks God that he is not like other sinners, including the man next to him. Part of his self-righteous claim is that he fasts twice a week and pays all the tithes he gets. Meanwhile, the tax collector won't even lift his eyes but cries out for mercy because he is a sinner. Jesus says this second man is the one who went home justified (Luke 18:9–14). God is looking for humble hearts, not perfect performance.

God addressed the same issues in the Old Testament. Isaiah 58:1–12 is an essential scripture passage on fasting. God's people are asking, "Why have we fasted and You do not see? Why have we humbled ourselves and You do not notice?" (Isa 58:3)

God proceeds to lay out their hypocrisy. They had become too focused on the rituals and lost sight of the meaning. They were offering sacrifices and going through the motions in a way that shined a spotlight on themselves, and then they expected to be rewarded for it.

But God tells them the fast He has chosen is to loosen the bonds of wickedness, to let the oppressed go free, and to serve the hungry and homeless. His promise is that:

> *Then your light will break out like the dawn, and your recovery will spring up quickly; and your righteousness will go before you; the glory of the Lord will be your rear guard.*
>
> *Then you will call, and the Lord will answer; you will cry for help, and He will say, 'Here I am.' If you remove the yoke from your midst, the pointing of the finger and speaking wickedness (Isa 58:8-9).*

Fasting shouldn't become a religious routine or an empty ritual. We can't look down on other people because they don't fast as much as we do or don't fast in the same way. We don't become more holy because we fast, and God doesn't love us any more than He already does based on whether or not we fast.

Second, a spiritual fast is not a weight loss diet. Intermittent fasting has become a popular method for losing weight, but that is a different plan, protocol, and motivation than when we fast for spiritual purposes. You may lose some weight while fasting, but you'll likely gain it all back if you return to your previous eating habits.

Weight loss is a complicated endeavor with genetics, environment, and daily habits all playing a role. While fasting can highlight our poor eating habits and help us make adjustments to those, we also have to transform our thinking around weight loss.

Being overweight or obese increases health risks, so it's good to maintain a healthy weight. At the same time, some people are on a perpetual diet not for health reasons, but to lose the elusive last ten pounds. We may be healthy, but we're convinced our bodies need to look a certain way in order for us to finally be attractive and satisfied with our appearance.

Food can easily become an idol in our lives. We can be in a constant battle to control food, but it feels like food is controlling us. Thoughts of what to eat, or not eat, can dominate our minds, and feelings of guilt over our eating habits can easily turn into deep shame. That shift happens when we don't just regret eating a second helping, but we condemn ourselves for being a terrible person with no self-control. It doesn't help that we can be hit with marketing to order fast food and exercise equipment within the same commercial break. Society has us constantly thinking about both what to eat and how to lose weight.

Here's a litmus test for your motivation: Would you feel the same way about losing weight if you had nobody to compare yourself to and if you never heard another marketing message about weight loss, exercise, and appearance?

Now is the time to decide that food, hunger, and your body are not your enemies. Learning to view food as fuel and to be enjoyed in moderation will bring you a new level of freedom. Eating to live is a healthier approach than living to eat. Fostering gratitude for your body and properly focusing on health will transform your mindset around eating.

Finally, don't be derailed by the temptation to quit your fast. Challenging circumstances and discouragement may come. You'll probably get hungry and feel weak at some point. Or you may decide to fast, then everything goes wrong. A stressful new project pops up at work, your kids are sick, the dog gets fleas, and you feel compelled to throw in the towel.

When these challenges come, negative thoughts can start popping up, such as I'm not cut out for this; other people have the discipline, but it's too hard for me; I better leave this to the really holy people; I picked the wrong time, so I'll try again next year; or I don't really need to do this anyway—since I'm already saved, there's no point in being this uncomfortable.

When these thoughts arise, you need to return to the original question: Why did I decide to fast? As you remind yourself of the purpose, you strengthen your resolve and commitment.

A similar mindset is required when starting an exercise program. To strengthen your muscles, you need to lift weights or perform strength-building exercises. If the weight is too light, it will feel easier and more comfortable, but you won't get any stronger. You have to challenge your current capacity and lift heavier weights in order to stress the muscle and increase strength.

The same applies when fasting. Fasting puts a gentle stress on our spirit, soul, and body that will ultimately strengthen us. It doesn't always feel easy, and the results aren't instantaneous, but we commit to trust the process and put value on long-term goals rather than short-term comfort.

Your Reasons for Fasting

The first time I had ever fasted was with my church. Our pastors called for a corporate time of prayer and fasting at the beginning of the year. I was intrigued. I had never participated in a fast before but was eager to take this step and see what God would do.

Corporate fasts are mentioned throughout the Bible, and it can be powerful to fast in community with others. But there is also fruit from pursuing a personal spiritual discipline of fasting during a time that's just between you and God. I have been prompted to fast at various times when seeking:

- Alignment with God
- Clarity in decision making
- Prayer for specific needs
- A spiritual tune-up when feeling distant or disengaged
- Greater intimacy with the Lord
- Strength through a challenging situation

So now it's time to consider why you picked up this book in the first place. You probably have some ideas about why fasting would benefit you. Before we dive into what the Bible says about fasting in the next section, take a few minutes to think about your motivations and purpose for fasting.

Your Journey

To summarize this chapter, fasting is a holistic practice that will impact your spirit, soul, and body. Every part will be involved. Fasting isn't about having a spiritually powered diet plan or twisting God's arm to get the results you want. You are already loved by God and He hears all your prayers.

Fasting does have many benefits for you. It's a pathway to grow even closer to the Lord. Paul told Timothy to discipline himself for the purpose of godliness (1 Tim 4:7). The word for discipline in this context is gymnazo which means to vigorously exercise the body or the mind.[XIII] Through fasting, we are exercising and maturing our faith, as we improve the health of our bodies.

Chapter 2 Reflections

• Do you feel like your spirit, soul, and body are in sync? If not, in what area do you most need to improve your health?

• Have you ever shifted your diet to eat primarily plant-based foods? If so, how did you feel, and if not, what do you think about this idea?

• What are your motivations for fasting? List all that apply. This is also a good time to go to danielfastjourney.com/bookresources and download your "Fasting Planning & Reflection Journal" if you haven't already done so.

PART TWO
REFRESH YOUR SPIRIT

Chapter 3

Study Your Map: What the Bible Says About Fasting

And Jesus said to them, "The attendants of the bridegroom cannot mourn as long as the bridegroom is with them, can they? But the days will come when the bridegroom is taken away from them, and then they will fast."—Matthew 9:15

Before we fast we must have a purpose, a God-centered purpose.
—Donald Whitney

When I first learned to drive, we didn't have smartphones and apps. Maybe you have this same memory. If we needed directions, we had to unfold a giant paper map to trace the route. When going to visit someone for the first time, we would write down step-by-step in-structions. We had to pay attention and remember to turn right by the school, go past the blue house with the orange fence, and stay on the lookout for other turns and landmarks.

Now, we can plug an address into our phone and mindlessly follow directions without worrying how many steps are required along the way. If we take a wrong turn, a reassuring robotic voice immediately corrects us with the notice: "recalculating route, make a U-turn."

Our technology isn't necessarily foolproof, however. Many times, I have been so deadlocked on obeying the voice in my phone that I ignored my intuition and turned left when I knew I should continue straight. Because I didn't take a few minutes on the front end to look through the entire route, I got sidetracked, and it ultimately took more time, effort, and stress to get where I was trying to go.

When it comes to fasting, we're often in the same boat (or car). We've decided to do a Daniel Fast and immediately jump to search for recipes. But that is like mindlessly following the automatic directions. We first need to survey what fasting entails from start to finish, not just for our particular plan but also for how fasting fits into the larger scope of the Bible. Although anecdotes and supplemental information can be helpful, nothing compares to searching the original source and examining what the Word of God says about fasting.

Old Testament Fasting

In the Old Testament, we see stories of people fasting in times of national crisis, while mourning, for repentance, and while seeking God. These fasts range from Daniel avoiding meat and wine to complete fasts of no food or water. We can see how God provided direction, protection, and comfort when people in need were seeking His will through prayer and fasting.

Battle and national crisis

An early mention of fasting is found in the book of Judges. The context is battle. In this unfortunate situation, the sons of Israel went to war against the tribe of Benjamin because of an unpardonable murder that demanded justice.

During the battle, the soldiers of Israel came to the Lord with weeping and offerings, "and thus they remained before the Lord and fasted that day until evening." (Judg 20:2) When they asked the Lord whether they should continue, He told them to go. He instructed the men of Israel to set up an ambush, and they were victorious. God not only gave them the assurance to press forward, He also gave a very specific strategy for how to fight and win this battle.

In another incident, the Ammonites and Moabites threatened the kingdom of Judah. Facing an immense threat, with multitudes coming in from beyond the sea, King Jehoshaphat called the entire nation to unite and turn to the Lord for guidance. In 2 Chronicles 20:3, we read that Jehoshaphat was afraid, and as he turned his attention to seek the Lord, he proclaimed a fast throughout all Judah.

King Jehoshaphat fought this battle spiritually as well as physically. He gathered all the people of Judah, including babies and infants, as he called on the Lord and prayed. In this assembly, the Spirit of the Lord came down and one of the Levites made this great proclamation:

"Do not fear or be dismayed because of this great multitude, for the battle is not yours but God's." (2 Chr 20:15)

Along with prayer and fasting, they also engaged in worship. As Judah marched into battle King Jehoshaphat "appointed those who sang to the Lord and those who praised Him in holy attire, as they went out before the army." (2 Chr 20:21) As this battle concluded, Judah's enemies were destroyed and the spoil was more than they could carry away.

Queen Esther is another leader who called for fasting in a time of crisis. While the Jews were in exile under the Persian Empire, Esther learned of a plot to destroy all Jews. Being a Jew herself, the only possibility of survival required Esther to go into the king to plead the case of the Jewish people . . . without being summoned. To approach the king unsummoned was a move punishable by death. But in this crisis, she had no alternative and no time to waste.

Esther called all the Jews in Susa to not eat or drink for three days, and she and her maidens would also fast at this same time (Est 4:16). She went to King Ahasuerus on the third day and not only was her life spared, but she was able to save the Jewish people and see justice served.

Although we may not face physical battles and death threats, we still confront a variety of enemies in our daily lives. Whether the attack is spiritual or manifesting through people and circumstances, do you take time to pray and fast before launching into battle?

In these particular examples, the leaders had the authority to call on the masses to engage in fasting and prayer. Even if you aren't in a political position, prayer and fasting is a powerful response to a national crisis. We are all called to intercede for justice, freedom for oppressed people, and for our governing officials.

Wisdom comes when we pause and seek the Lord first before we react. Whether it's a larger national crisis or a personal battle that you're facing, it's easy to get swept up in chaos and confusion. We need the Lord's covering and protection physically and mentally. We also need divine wisdom for our offensive strategy. Consider the favor in each of the examples above when the problem was taken to the Lord first. The leaders were victorious because of divinely inspired plans and tactics.

Mourning

In the Bible, people fasted in times of distress and mourning. Fasting was often accompanied by demonstrative weeping and putting on sackcloth and ashes. One example is when the men of Israel fasted for seven days after burying King Saul and his son Jonathan (1 Sam 31:13).

Nehemiah was devastated when he heard the news that the walls of Jerusalem had been broken down. In this time, having strong walls around a city was vital for safety and protection. His response was to sit down and weep and mourn for several days. During this time, he was fasting and praying to God, mourning over a dire situation for his people (Neh 1:4). With the walls of Jerusalem broken down, the city was exposed, and people were vulnerable. After this emotional time spent seeking the Lord, Nehemiah ultimately rose up, petitioned the king for travel and supplies, and led the team who would rebuild the wall in fifty-two days.

Repentance

In the Old Testament, people also responded with mourning and fasting when they were convicted of sin. Repentance means changing the mind. It's one action with two parts: to stop going in one direction and start moving in another. While sin leads you in a direction of increasing separation from God, repentance is the decision to turn around and move back towards Him.

When people were engaging in sin, the prophet Joel delivered a strong message from God, calling the people to announce a time of fasting. " 'Yet even now,' declares the Lord, 'Return to Me with all your heart, and with fasting, weeping and mourning; and rend your heart and not your garments.' Now return to the Lord your God." (Joel 2:12–13) God is seeking a true heart change through fasting.

After Jonah preached to Nineveh, the people of the city called a fast and put on sackcloth. The king did the same and issued a proclamation that no man or beast should eat or drink, but that each should turn from their wicked ways and honor God (Jon 3:8). The prophet's message pierced the hearts of the people, and they all responded.

Seeking God

Whether faced with a threat, a tragedy, or conviction of your own sin, certain moments shake your assumption of self-sufficiency. When you're at the end of your rope with nowhere else to turn, God can step in and provide the answers you need.

In addition to the examples already listed, here are some more instances of people seeking the Lord with fasting:

• David was struck with grief for his son who was near death. "David therefore inquired of God for the child; and David fasted and went and lay all night on the ground." (2 Sam 12:16)

• Hannah desperately wanted a child, and wept and did not eat as she prayed and "poured out [her] soul before the Lord." (1 Sam 1:15)

• Daniel was convicted for the sins and iniquities of his people as he read the book of Jeremiah. "So I gave my attention to the Lord God to seek Him by prayer and supplications, with fasting, sackcloth, and ashes." (Dan 9:3)

• The Israelites needed direction when returning from exile to Jerusalem to rebuild the temple, "So we fasted and sought our God concerning this [matter] and He listened to our entreaty." (Ezra 8:23)

New Testament Fasting

There are significant mentions of fasting in the New Testament, starting with the birth of Jesus. A widow named Anna was in the temple when Jesus was presented as a baby. She is called a prophetess, and the gospel says she never left the temple but served around the clock with fasting and prayer. When she saw the baby, she immediately recognized that the infant Jesus was the Messiah. She gave thanks to God and continued to speak about Him to everyone in Jerusalem (Luke 2:36–38).

Although fasting was sometimes a response to anguish and mourning, here is a beautiful picture of a joyful life devoted to worship, prayer, and fasting! Embracing fasting as an act of worship and part of her spiritual rhythm, Anna was close to God and sensitive to His spirit, which enabled her to instantly recognize Jesus.

The book of Acts shows us the lives of Jesus's apostles and followers immediately following His death and ascension into heaven. The church began with people who referred to themselves as "disciples of the Lord" and followers of "the Way" (Acts 19:23). Acts 11:26 says the disciples were first called Christians at Antioch.

They united as a family, a community with common principles and values. This is the birth of the church. These believers established the first example of gathering, worshiping, and walking out their faith. Along with these other practices, fasting was a regular part of their lives.

As the leaders of the church fasted and worshiped together, the Holy Spirit instructed them to set Barnabas and Saul (Paul) apart. So they fasted, prayed, laid hands on them, and sent them on their way (Acts 13:2–3). As they were sent out by the Holy Spirit, they were empowered in both direction and mission.

If you have a decision to make, these scriptures from the book of

Acts should be especially encouraging. God wants to guide you. As Paul and Barnabas traveled, they "appointed elders in every church, and prayed with fasting, they commended them to the Lord in whom they believed." (Acts 14:23)

Fasting is again used as a ministry tool and for the benefit of others. When we fast and pray, we're not just looking introspectively to improve our own condition but also looking up and out so we impact others in our sphere of influence with God's will and strategies at the forefront of our minds. As you fast, consider how you can do good to others, encourage them, and pray for them.

Supernatural encounters occurred during times of prayer and fasting. Saul (who was later called Paul) was traveling to Damascus to look for Christians, known as followers of "the Way," to imprison them. He had an encounter with the Lord, and Jesus spoke to him and directed him to visit Ananias, a disciple who was living in Damascus. Saul fasted for three days and was unable to see.

During this same time, the Lord told Ananias in a vision that he · should lay hands on Saul. Although he was apprehensive because of Saul's reputation and the previous harm he had done, when the two men met, they had both heard from God and obeyed His supernatural direction. After Ananias laid hands on Saul, something like scales fell from his eyes and he was able to see, and he took food and was strengthened (see Acts 9:1–19).

Another divine encounter occurs in Acts Chapter 10. Cornelius was a Roman centurion who worshiped God. As he was praying and fasting, God told him to send for Peter. Simultaneously, Peter received a vision from God that was symbolic of God's will to preach the gospel to all people, not only Jews but also Gentiles.

With this preface, when Peter was called to the house of this Roman soldier, the Spirit directed him to go. As Peter preached the gospel to this family, the Holy Spirit fell on everyone listening with power, and the entire household was saved (see Acts 10:1–48).

This is not an exhaustive list of every mention of fasting in the Bible. You can find a list of scripture references to diet, food, and fasting in the appendix, and I encourage you to take your own time in Bible study to read more.

Your Journey

These biblical examples have a key thread in common. In every circumstance, people are seeking God for His will and direction. Fasting is often a response to distress, accompanied by strong emotion and a desperation for answers. Our world would look significantly different if our first response to trouble was to turn to God with prayer and fasting instead of gravitating towards food, alcohol, technology, or other addictive substances.

Continue to pray and dive deeper into God's word for encouragement and revelation on fasting and consider what this means for your own life.

Chapter 3 Reflections

• Are any of the stories in this chapter new to you? Look up those verses to read the story in full context.

• Do you see any examples of fasting without prayer? Why do you think prayer plays such a vital role?

• How do you think fasting was different in the church in the book of Acts compared to today?

Chapter 4

Consult Your Guides: How Daniel and Jesus Fasted

Jesus, full of the Holy Spirit, returned from the Jordan and was led around by the Spirit in the wilderness for forty days, being tempted by the devil. And He ate nothing during those days, and when they had ended, He became hungry.

—Luke 4:1–2

Bear up the hands that hang down, by faith and prayer; support the tottering knees. Have you any days of fasting and prayer? Storm the throne of grace and persevere therein, and mercy will come down.—John Wesley

In the last chapter, we covered many examples of fasting throughout the Old and New Testaments. Now it's time to consider the example of two key biblical figures. When you're taking part in a Daniel Fast, it's essential to study the stories of Daniel and Jesus and see how they fasted personally.

Daniel had an extraordinary spirit and prayer life. He was a foreign exile and counselor to several kings throughout his lifetime. He faced intense pressure, conflict with enemies, and multiple threats against his life. Yet Daniel always went to God first for guidance and protection.

Daniel not only trusted the Lord when in danger, but he also praised Him when things went well. Daniel honored the people around him, even if the situation was corrupt and he had to object. As a result, he rose in influence and was promoted several times throughout his life by different kings and rulers. Despite his worldly success, he remained fully devoted to and dependent on God.

Over the years, I have found myself repeatedly returning to the book of Daniel. It's been one of my greatest inspirations, especially in the arena of leadership. When I read about his life, I can hardly relate to some of the serious challenges he faced. My struggles are real, but I've never worried about anything as life-threatening as a fiery furnace or lion's den or being executed because I couldn't interpret my boss's dream.

Daniel's legacy extends beyond the fasting practice we've named after him. When an angelic messenger comes to visit Daniel, he tells him, "Do not be afraid, Daniel, for from the first day that you set your heart on understanding this and on humbling yourself before your God, your words were heard, and I have come in response to your words." (Dan 10:12)

To gain understanding, remain humble, and pray continuously . . . this describes Daniel's character. His prayers reverberated through heaven and earth because of who he was. His life is a picture of an intimate connection to the Father.

Before we step into our Daniel Fast, let's take a look at the scope of Daniel's life. His motivation and relationship with the Lord are more important than the list of what he ate. Throughout his life, Daniel's commitment to the Lord was demonstrated in his spiritual disciplines, personal choices, and exceptional character.

The Life of Daniel

The book of Daniel begins when Neo-Babylonian King Nebuchadnezzar seized Jerusalem and transported captives and plunder to Babylon around 605 BC. Daniel and his friends, teenagers at the time, were among those who were taken. The first six chapters of the book of Daniel are a chronological account of events. The last six chapters describe Daniel's dreams and visions. Here is a brief overview of these first six chapters.

Daniel and his friends were brought into the king's personal service when they arrived in Babylon. They were the best of the best, most likely from the wealthier and better-educated families of Jerusalem society. The Bible says they had no defect, were good-looking, showed intelligence in every branch of wisdom, were endowed with understanding and discerning knowledge, and had the ability to serve in the king's court. The next step for their assimilation into the culture was to teach them the literature and language of the Chaldeans (Dan 1:4).

During this indoctrination period, Daniel resolved not to defile himself with the king's food and wine. In verse twelve he asks the head of the guard to test him and his friends by giving them only vegetables and water. He doesn't refer to it as a fast (although this is the foundation for our modern Daniel Fast). The Hebrew word translated as test means "to prove." And I believe he was testing to prove that God would be his source and strength no matter what.

Historians say Daniel most likely abstained because of concerns about idol worship and the origin of the meat he would be eating. He was also determined to avoid drunkenness and honor God's explicit laws for a kosher diet. Whatever his reasons, Daniel was committed.

In the end, they certainly passed the ten-day test with flying colors. Their appearance seemed better, and they were fatter than any of the other youths. Based on the results, they were able to continue receiving the same all-vegetable diet going forward.

God blessed them with knowledge, intelligence, and wisdom in everything they studied, and Daniel even understood visions and dreams. When they were presented to King Nebuchadnezzar at the end of this training, he was thoroughly impressed. These four boys who were tested for ten days were in fact "ten times better." (Dan 1:20)

Chapter one concludes by saying that Daniel continued until the first year of Cyrus the king. This means he was away from his homeland for seventy years! He served under King Nebuchadnezzar,

Belshazzar, Darius the Mede, and Cyrus the Persian. This mention is also significant because Cyrus was the king who allowed the Jews to return to Jerusalem, so Daniel was there from the beginning to the end of the exile.

Daniel interpreted a significant dream for King Nebuchadnezzar in chapter two that comes to pass in chapter four. Nebuchadnezzar loses his sanity for a period of time until he humbles himself and honors God. We'll cover more details of this encounter in the next section on Daniel's prayer life.

In chapter three, we read the well-known story of Shadrach, Meshach, and Abednego and the fiery furnace. Nebuchadnezzar constructed a gold statue on the plain of Dura and assembled all the judges, magistrates, satraps, and other officials. They were ordered to fall down and worship the golden image when they heard the music, but these three boys refused.

As punishment, they were thrown into the furnace that was heated seven times hotter than normal. This was certain death, but a miracle occurred. A fourth man appeared in the fire with them, and they emerged with no damage, not even the smell of smoke. Completely amazed, Nebuchadnezzar made a decree that nobody could harm them, so they prospered in the province of Babylon.

In chapter five, Nebuchadnezzar's son Belshazzar and his nobles were drinking wine from the goblets that had been plundered from the temple in Jerusalem when a hand appeared and wrote a mysterious message on the wall. (Can you imagine how much that dampened the party vibe?) As everyone sat in shock, the king's wife remembered Daniel and his gifts and brought him in to interpret the message.

There are more details in this story, but in summary, the message interpretation and what came to pass was that because Belshazzar did not humble himself and honor God, his days were numbered and the kingdom would be stripped away. He was killed that very night and a regime change takes place with Darius the Mede coming into power.

Belshazzar gave orders to clothe Daniel in purple and put a chain around his neck right before he was slain. He gave Daniel authority as the third ruler in the kingdom. When Darius becomes ruler, he appoints three commissioners to oversee the satraps (officials) in the kingdom, and Daniel is one of the three.

At this time, "Daniel began distinguishing himself among the commissioners and satraps because he possessed an extraordinary spirit, and the king planned to appoint him over the entire kingdom." (Dan 6:3) Upset and disgruntled, the other commissioners and satraps began plotting against him. But they couldn't find a single accusation because he was neither corrupt nor negligent.

Not only was his character above moral reproach, but he also wasn't neglecting a single detail at work. He hadn't dropped any balls or cut any corners. So to convict Daniel, his opponents would have to set a trap and make accusations based on his faith. They convinced Darius to sign a statute requiring people to pray to the king alone, and the penalty was to be thrown in the lions' den.

Daniel was not swayed by threats and politics. He went to his roof chamber that had windows open towards Jerusalem, and "he continued kneeling on his knees three times a day, praying and giving thanks before his God as he had done previously." (Dan 6:10)

The king was deeply grieved when he heard the news but had to follow through and throw Daniel in the lions' den because he couldn't go back on his word. Daniel was placed in the lions' den, and a stone was rolled to block the entrance. Meanwhile, the king was up all night fasting and could not sleep.

Darius went to the den at dawn to find Daniel alive with no injuries because God had sent an angel to shut the lions' mouths. His accusers and their families were thrown into the den instead. Darius makes a decree honoring the God of Daniel and Daniel enjoyed success throughout his reign and in the reign of Cyrus the Persian.

You may see the parallels in the story of the lions' den to the story of the death, burial, and resurrection of Jesus. Jesus also had jealous enemies who plotted against him. As they tried to trap him and find a reason to convict him, they could only accuse him based on the statements he made concerning His faith. Although Jesus was sealed in a tomb and left for dead, when the women went to attend to Him at dawn, they found that He was alive (see Matt 27-28).

Before we examine Jesus's example and teaching on fasting, let's finish up the book of Daniel. Throughout his life, Daniel had incredible visions of heavenly messengers and future events. He also has supernatural insight into practical and political matters. These divine revelations were all tied to his lifestyle of prayer and fasting.

Daniel's Lifestyle of Prayer and Fasting

Daniel and his friends had many choices to make about lifestyle, assimilation, and values when they were taken captive and brought to Babylon. Their choices affected more than popularity or ascending the political ladder—the consequence could literally be death. They came face to face with that risk multiple times, as we just discussed.

Despite the threats, every time Daniel had to decide to either go along with culture or make a stand for faith, he chose to stand. Daniel also blended practical wisdom, timing, and interpersonal skills with supernatural gifts and revelations from God. We get a peek into some of these revelations in the first half of the book of Daniel and a full picture in the second half.

In the second chapter of Daniel, King Nebuchadnezzar had a disturbing dream. He brought in his magicians, sorcerers, and conjurers and demanded that they tell him both the dream and its interpretation. When they declared this was an impossible task, the king was furious and ordered that all the wise men were to be slain.

Bad news for Daniel and his friends. Even though they weren't present at the palace, they were included in this group of advisors and, therefore, subject to the death sentence. Rather than react with fear and panic, Daniel replied with discretion and discernment. He requested more time from the king.

How did Daniel spend this time? He didn't spin his wheels brainstorming and strategizing an escape plan. He didn't debate at length with his friends. He only asked them to pray and request compassion from God. Then Daniel spent the night in prayer, seeking answers from the Lord.

And God gave him the revelation that saved their lives. With overwhelming humility, Daniel took no credit; instead, he praised the Lord. His focal point was not his own gifts or ability to interpret the dream, but God's goodness and faithfulness.

Daniel stewarded every opportunity he was given, and his influence expanded. Daniel was promoted after his initial training (when he and his friends were found ten times better than everyone else), at the end of chapter two, by Belshazzar at the end of chapter five, and was one of three commissioners appointed by Darius the Mede in chapter six.

In chapter seven, Daniel recounts a dream and vision he had in the first year of Belshazzar's reign. He has a revelation of the throne of the Ancient of Days and the heavenly court as well as of the Son of Man. In this chapter and the ones that follow, he receives revelation about the rise and fall of earthly kingdoms and rulers and speaks with the angel Gabriel, as he does on other occasions. Despite the awesomeness of what he sees, he keeps these visions secret as instructed.

Chapters two and six show us a glimpse of Daniel's prayer life. Prayer was his first response to a crisis and a regular, intentional habit. Although he prayed in the privacy of his home, his commitment was obvious to those around him—so evident that they were able to set a trap based on the times he was known to be in prayer.

Although these supernatural encounters sound amazing, they also took a physical and emotional toll on Daniel. After his vision in chapter eight, the word says that he was exhausted and sick for days. Even as he got up and went back to work, he was astounded at the vision and nobody was able to explain it (Dan 8:27). There were other points when Daniel fell down, expressed fear, and experienced exhaustion.

Although the Daniel Fast is based on chapter 1 of the book of Daniel, the second half of this book references two other periods when Daniel fasted.

In the first year of Darius, Daniel read the book of Jeremiah referencing the seventy years of captivity and was driven to the Lord "to seek Him by prayer and supplications, with fasting, sackcloth and ashes." (Dan 9:3) He prayed and confessed his own sin and the sins of his people which had led to their exile, pleading with God on their behalf.

Daniel also fasted for twenty-one days during the third year of Cyrus. During this time Daniel, "did not eat any tasty food, nor did meat or wine enter [his] mouth, nor did [he] use any ointment at all until the entire three weeks were completed." (Dan 10:2)

It's important to note, Daniel wasn't fasting for the purpose of seeking supernatural encounters. His fasting was anchored in his relationship with God and, coupled with prayer, was a response to distress. These supernatural encounters were a byproduct of his actions. A regular devotion to prayer preceded dreams and visions. God surely trusted Daniel with this secret knowledge because of his attitude and habits over the years.

If you're not already familiar with the book of Daniel, I hope that hearing about his life inspires you to dig in and study more. His life has a much greater impact than motivating us to a ten-day, vegetable-only fast. He shows us what it looks like to live a life fully devoted to God, worshiping Him no matter the consequences or challenges.

Jesus and Fasting

Jesus is the cornerstone of the Christian faith, and as His disciples, we are called to live like Him, paying close attention to what He taught. Jesus completed a forty-day fast in the wilderness before He entered full-time ministry at the age of thirty. At the end of this fast, He was tempted by the devil but emerged victoriously.

Jesus made several references to fasting. In Matthew chapter six, Jesus teaches His disciples about three key spiritual disciplines: giving, praying, and fasting. He doesn't position them as suggestions. In all three instances, he does not propose, "if you *choose*" but declares "when you *do*." As a follower of Jesus, we are called to give, pray, and fast.

I haven't met anyone who would dismiss the importance of praying and giving to those in need. But fasting . . . that's a different story! Fasting is undoubtedly taught and practiced the least of the three.

Why is fasting so challenging? Fasting requires us to give up two things we hold dear: comfort and control. I don't believe fasting would be so difficult and contested by both our flesh and the enemy unless it was extremely powerful. Jesus Himself fasted, and also gave specific instruction about fasting we can personally apply today.

How Jesus Fasted

The Bible doesn't record details of Jesus's life from age twelve to thirty. We assume he worked and grew up like any other boy during that time. As an adult, Jesus came to his cousin John to be water baptized. At this time, "the heavens were opened, and he saw the Spirit of God descending as a dove [and] lighting on Him, and behold, a voice out of the heavens said, 'This is My beloved Son, in whom I am well-pleased.'" (Matt 3:16–17)

In this moment we see the Trinity together: Jesus is walking the earth as the Son of Man; God is speaking, and the Spirit is moving. With this affirmation from His Father, Jesus entered a period of fasting. The Bible tells us He was led by the Spirit into the wilderness and fasted forty days and forty nights (Matt 4:1–2).

After this time, Jesus entered full-time ministry, so we can be sure that whatever transpired was foundational for his next step. I wish we had a glimpse into these forty days! How was Jesus praying? What was He thinking? What secrets did the Father reveal to Him during this time? Whatever transpired, this fast marked a significant turning point in His life.

While fasting, Jesus experienced hunger and was tempted by the devil who questioned his identity and provision on three levels. (This story is relayed in the gospels of Matthew, Mark, and Luke.) Three times the devil came to Jesus and posed the question, "If you are the Son of God . . ."

The first time the enemy tempted him to command the stones to become bread, the second time to throw Himself down from the pinnacle of the temple and be caught by angels, and the third time to bow down and worship him to receive all the kingdoms of the world and their glory (Matt 4:1–14).

These temptations have been referred to as hedonism, egoism, and materialism. This is an attempt to corrupt the thoughts, wishes, and feelings residing in the mind, soul, and heart.[XIV] The first epistle of John summarizes the sins of the world as "the lust of the flesh and the lust of the eyes and the boastful pride of life." (1John 2:16)

Jesus was both fully God and fully man and faced all the temptations humans experience. When the devil planted doubt in the garden ("Did God really say . . . ") Adam and Eve gave in to temptation, but Jesus stood against the enemy when tempted. He did not doubt His identity as the son of God. In His life, death, and resurrection, Jesus overcame the curse of the fall and the death that resulted when Adam and Eve disobeyed God and ate the fruit from the tree of knowledge of good and evil.

Jesus's offensive weapon against the tempter was the word of God. Something that should catch our attention in this story is that the enemy used scripture to rationalize his questions and proposals. But Jesus rebuked him with scripture in the right context. Jesus demonstrated why it's so vital to not just be familiar with a few Bible verses but to study the Bible in-depth for full context and understanding. Without the foundational word of God, it would be easy to be distracted, led astray by false teaching, or confused about the truth.

What Did Jesus Say About Fasting

Jesus didn't just provide a personal example of fasting, He also spoke specifically about what it means to fast. We don't have to guess what He thought since we have some specific teaching. Here are some of the instructions He gave to guide us in fasting.

How you fast

Jesus is clear that fasting is not for ritual or for show. Like many religious practices during His time, there was a gap between the letter of the law and the spirit of the law. In other words, focusing on what to do while ignoring *why* and *how* to do it.

And this same gap can exist today. For example, what happens when you tell your child to clean their room and they stomp upstairs, bang around, and shove everything under the bed?

Did they complete the goal?

Technically, yes, but they missed the mark when it comes to method. The purpose is to care for your belongings and provide order, not just to clear the floor and make sure everyone knows how miserable you are while doing it!

Likewise, we can fall into this same trap spiritually. Jesus taught His followers to look beyond the rituals and focus on building a relationship. It's not about checking the box and making a public demonstration for man's approval. He told them:

> Whenever you fast, do not put on a gloomy face as the hypocrites do, for they neglect their appearance so that they will be noticed by men when they are fasting. Truly I say to you, they have their reward in full. But you, when you fast, anoint your head and wash your face so that your fasting will not be noticed by men, but by your Father who is in secret; and your Father who sees what is done in secret will reward you. (Matt 6:17–18)

We see the promise of a blessing. Before you get too excited, remember God's definition of reward can be very different from the world's. It's not necessarily a mansion on the beach in Hawaii, the praise of people, or an immediate payday. God's reward is a heavenly promise, and you may have to wait for it.

Are you willing to trust that God is really enough? Jesus says to anoint your head and wash your face because fasting is not a miserable experience. In fact, you may feel more "full" than you ever have before. Full of life, full of energy, full of the Spirit. Although you thought you needed food to fill you up, God has something better in store.

When you fast

When Jesus taught and ministered, He constantly challenged the status quo thinking of His time. Although our modern world has different cultural norms compared to biblical times, surrendering your life to Jesus is still a radical shift. As you follow Christ, you navigate a variety of expectations and opinions. On one hand, there are various denominational and traditional religious expectations. On the other are the differing opinions and viewpoints from what is commonly accepted in popular culture.

Jesus and His disciples experienced these same tensions. His teachings often provoked both the Pharisees and religious leaders, and also challenged the people listening to His messages. One thing that was unsettling to the religious leaders of the day was their practice of fasting—or more accurately, not fasting. Passages from three different gospels recount the following scene.[xv]

The disciples of John and the Pharisees noticed that the disciples of Jesus were not fasting as they did, according to custom. When they inquired why, Jesus compared Himself to a bridegroom and said that as long as the bridegroom is with the attendants, they cannot mourn. Jesus clarified, "But the days will come when the bridegroom is taken away from them, and then they will fast in that day." (Mark 2:20)

Immediately following the question about fasting, Jesus shares an example of not sewing a new piece of cloth onto an old garment or pouring new wine into old wineskins. "No one tears a piece of cloth from a new garment and puts it on an old garment; otherwise he will both tear the new, and the piece from the new will not match the old." (Luke 5:36)

If the goal of fasting is to grow closer to the Lord, the disciples didn't need to fast when Jesus was physically present with them. But later, when He was gone, fasting would be necessary to continue to separate from the world and view things from a heavenly, eternal, and Christ-centered perspective. Essentially, they wouldn't be able to settle back into old, brittle ways of religion, they would need open hearts ready for new methods and fresh messages from God.

Again, Jesus presents the issue of fasting not as a matter of *if*, but *when* His followers would fast. The metaphor of Jesus as a bridegroom and the church as the bride is used throughout the New Testament. The church, as a body of believers, is called to prepare for this special day when Jesus will be reunited with His bride.

Why you fast

In a later story, Jesus came down from the mountain and encountered a distraught father. This man's son was suffering, tormented by a demon that was causing him physical and mental pain (see Matt 17:14-20 and Mk 9:14-29).

When Jesus arrived, he commanded the spirit to come out and the boy was healed. And the disciples asked Him: Why couldn't we do it?

Jesus's answer was that you need faith, prayer, and fasting. He told them that faith even as small as a mustard seed can move a mountain, and nothing is impossible. He stood next to a literal mountain, the one He was transfigured on, as He offered this illustration but He wasn't referring to literal, physical objects.

We face spiritual mountains, obstacles, and difficulties, and these spiritual battles must be fought with spiritual weapons. After talking about the fundamental and foundational faith required, He added, "But this kind does not go out except by prayer and fasting." (Matt 17:21 NKJV) Although some translations end this statement with "prayer" and do not include "and fasting," I believe fasting is very applicable to our spiritual battles as both a tool and weapon for victory. When you are in a serious trial, drawing closer to God through fasting is a way to experience a breakthrough in the spiritual realm.

You may think . . . but I have tried this. I have prayed and fasted and I still did not move my spiritual mountain. Am I to blame because my faith is lacking or because I haven't prayed and fasted enough? Absolutely not! Sometimes we pray diligently and passionately and don't receive the answer we want. God tells us, "My thoughts are not your thoughts, nor are your ways my ways." (Isa 55:8) We don't always understand God's timing or method, but we can trust Him with the outcome.

Jesus clarified that this isn't about what you can do. You can't work miracles and wonders through your own power, strength, and skills. God is the one who heals and delivers, so your results are going to come by supernatural faith. When it happens, give God all the glory for the outcome, remembering how Daniel and Jesus praised God in every situation.

God controls the outcome, but you need to take a step of faith, using prayer and fasting as a highway connecting the natural and supernatural. In this world, we encounter very real pain, conflict, and suffering that cannot be ignored. But our job is to look beyond the physical obstacles in front of us and see the spiritual mountains behind them that must be addressed by faith and prayer.

You have the authority of Jesus as a believer. You have the sword of the Spirit which is the word of God and the power of the name of Jesus. Be confident that these are the weapons you need in warfare, and the enemy absolutely cannot stand against them.

Hold onto Jesus's promise that "this kind" will go out by prayer and fasting. You are not meant to live a heavy life in bondage, stuck fighting the same issues year after year. God wants your complete healing and freedom.

We'll find perfect wholeness someday in heaven, but we are also commissioned to bring heaven to earth. We are called to be overwhelming conquerors through Christ (Rom 8:37). Jesus told us, "The thief comes only to steal, kill, and destroy; I came that they may have life and have it abundantly." (John 10:10)

Build a community

Just like Jesus always traveled and did ministry with a group, nobody should go into battle alone but flanked on the right side, left side, and behind. Healthy community is always critical but especially so when you're walking through challenging times. It's difficult to thrive alone. Be honest and transparent with trusted counselors and friends so they can give you a balanced perspective and support you on your fasting journey.

Following the Pattern of Jesus

As you develop your personal practice of fasting, consider some of the reasons Jesus fasted. He showed us how fasting can prepare us, deepen our intimacy with God, and give us supernatural insight and power. Along with forty days of fasting before beginning His ministry, Jesus repeatedly spent time alone with His Father so He could continue to minister effectively to people.

Jesus told His disciples they would not only do the works He did but "greater works than these." (John 14:12) To operate in this capacity, we need to follow Jesus's pattern and take time for preparation and prayer.

Jesus said we should fast in secret so that only our heavenly Father sees because fasting is a time for communion and communication with God. While we don't know exactly what God told Jesus during his forty days in the wilderness, we know His presence was with him and will also be with us. God has unique things to say to you, specific to your personality, calling, and situation, but you have to take the time to listen. Your relationship with God will mature and grow in depth when you devote time and attention to Him.

He said this will even result in a spiritual reward. Jesus suffered and died so we could have a whole and abundant life. We have to receive by faith what He has given us and we do need to listen and make time for God. Four keys to victory that Jesus modeled for us are:

- Being still in the Lord's presence to listen and receive.

• Becoming less independent and self-reliant and more dependent on the Lord.

• Studying the word of God to learn His will.

• Sharpening our discernment and learning to recognize God's voice as we spend time in His presence.

Because of His time with the Father, Jesus could confidently say, "I can do nothing on my own initiative. As I hear, I judge; and my judgment is just, because I do not seek my own will, but the will of Him who sent me." (John 5:30)

Our spiritual vision grows sharper when we pray and fast. We begin to see things in a new way. Our prayers become more powerful. We move from personal requests for comfort to a kingdom mindset that calls for the Lord's will to be done on earth as it is in heaven. Healing, freedom, and health will all result as we fast.

Your Journey

As you prepare to fast, study the lives of Daniel and Jesus for encouragement and confirmation of the power of fasting for all believers. Whenever you take part in a Daniel Fast, it's beneficial to revisit these stories. The book of Daniel is just twelve chapters, but full of insight on how to live, worship God, and endure trials. Reading Jesus's words on fasting will also encourage you on how and why you should fast.

Chapter 4 Reflections

• Has your faith ever been challenged like Daniel and his friends, and if so, how did you handle it?

• Consider Jesus's example of fasting and what He taught about it. Take some time to read through the following three passages and ask the Holy Spirit for insight and a takeaway from each.

Luke 4:1–13
Matthew 6:16–21
Matthew 9:14–17

As you've read about the lives of Daniel and Jesus, has this changed your view on fasting in any way, and if so, how?

PART THREE
RENEW YOUR MIND

Chapter 5

Soul Food: Spiritual Disciplines While Fasting

Therefore I urge you, brethren, by the mercies of God, to present your bodies a living and holy sacrifice, acceptable to God, which is your spiritual service of worship. And do not be conformed to this world, but be transformed by the renewing of your mind, so that you may prove what the will of God is, that which is good and acceptable and perfect.—Rom 12:1–2

This is surely the loftiest conception, that fasting is a worshiping or ministering to the Lord, a giving of ourselves to God, and only secondarily a means to securing certain spiritual ends.—Arthur Wallis

A few weeks into kindergarten, I asked my daughter what her favorite subject was and what she liked best about school, and she replied, "Playground."

"You mean recess?" I clarified, but her response was the same:

playground. I probed about things she was learning in the classroom, what her teacher talked about, or whether her favorite subject was art or music. Even as I asked the question from different angles, she refused to budge from this one determined answer: playground. That was, she claimed, the only part of her day she enjoyed.

I can understand her answer given her high energy, active, and social personality. But no matter how much she prefers it, she needs more substance to her school day than just recess. Elementary students are oblivious to grown-up responsibilities like paying taxes, voting, and composing professional e-mails. Teachers and parents, on the other hand, are aware of the variety of skills these little ones will need when they grow up.

Whether or not it's fun and exciting, it's critical to study, practice, and develop foundational skills. The same principle remains true for us as adults who are maturing in our faith. Sometimes we don't know what we don't know, or what we may enjoy doing, unless we purposely seek to grow in knowledge and experience.

Fasting helps us grow, but it's one piece of the spiritual development puzzle. As we set aside time to fast, it's important to consider incorporating some other key spiritual disciplines. When we fast, we seek the revelation and transformation that comes from filling our lives with God's presence and power. This typically happens when we spend time with God, praying and reading His word.

When we fast, we take away physical food but supplement with spiritual food. Along with creating shopping lists and meal plans, we also need to prepare a space and develop a routine for spending time with God.

You may already have a strong preference for how you feel closest to God. Some prefer quiet contemplation, while others enjoy gathering in groups. Some people may enjoy extended times of prayer, while others are fulfilled by actively serving people. Most people are not naturally excited about fasting, but hopefully, that story will change.

Because we are wired uniquely, we're going to have particular preferences. But this doesn't excuse us from being obedient to all God has asked us to do. We're going to miss out if we only choose recess. We have to seek, study, and ask questions to unveil all God has for us to experience in our relationship with Him.

One of the teachers of the law asked Jesus which commandment is the greatest. He didn't respond with an action that can be easily measured. Jesus answered, "The foremost is, 'Hear, O Israel! The Lord our God is one Lord; and you shall love the Lord your God with all your heart, and with all your soul, and with all your mind, and with all your strength.'" And He adds the second greatest commandment, which is to love your neighbor as yourself (Mark 12:29–31).

This commandment is simple but not easy. It's direct but multifaceted. It's a tall order to love God with absolutely every part of your being. We don't get to pick and choose what feels easiest, most comfortable, or best suited to our personality, but if we put in the effort, we'll discover new things about God and ourselves. You can start with a very simple question. Just ask the Lord, "God, how can I know you better?"

Discipline

Fasting is only one piece of the puzzle. I love puzzles of all kinds, especially traditional jigsaw puzzles. It's smooth sailing when you're working out the border of straight edges, but then comes the monotonous work of filling in the sky or the grass of the landscape. Those are the sections where you need the most help and may be tempted to just sweep everything back in the box, but the picture won't be beautifully complete unless you're willing to be patient and keep plodding along.

In the same way, we tend to start strong with the obvious and easier parts of our spiritual journey but drift away when the work feels monotonous and less exciting. God doesn't want us to only dive in for the easy and preliminary steps of our faith, He wants us to get the whole picture because as the pieces fill in, the picture becomes clearer . . . and more beautiful.

When it comes to spiritual disciplines, we can't pick and choose which pieces we like; we need them all. Spiritual disciplines are practices that help us experience God, mature in our faith, and maintain a lifestyle that puts God first. The book of Acts shows the early church engaging in key habits like prayer, worship, gathering together, studying God's word, giving, serving, and fasting. This example continues throughout the New Testament and church history.

You may have a strong relationship with God. Perhaps you've studied the Bible for years and can easily explain theological concepts. Maybe you spend time with God daily and know what it means to feel close to Him and hear His voice. Or maybe you don't. Churchgoers can casually throw around phrases like "quiet time" and "reading the Word" without ever defining them, leaving new believers confused but hesitant to ask questions.

Are you supposed to read the Bible every day? How much should you read? Where should you start? What does it mean when you say God talks to you; do you actually hear a voice?

Rest assured, there isn't a step-by-step formula to follow or a grading rubric for measuring spiritual maturity. It doesn't look the same for everyone, and this chapter isn't about outlining a list of obligations and boxes to check daily. God loves us unconditionally, and we are saved by grace. Legalism would lead us to think we must earn our righteousness or prove our holiness through the works we do, which is not true.

However, for too many of us modern churchgoers, our efforts to avoid legalism can cause us to shy away from anything that feels too difficult, routine, or obligatory. But if we don't put in the effort to be disciplined, this can result in a faith that is passive, lacking passion and power. Having the discipline to show up consistently and pursue godly habits, even when we don't feel like it, is crucial for growth.

There is a difference between legalism and discipline; the two should not be confused. You can tell the difference by the spirit of the action and the results. Legalism focuses on the process, relies on the strength of man, and leads us towards bondage and man-made systems. Discipline focuses on the person, relies on God, and leads us towards freedom and the heavenly kingdom.

Hebrews 12:11 says, "All discipline for the moment seems not to be joyful, but sorrowful; yet to those who have been trained by it, afterwards it yields the peaceful fruit of righteousness." By definition, discipline is for the purpose of correction, teaching, and learning. The Latin word *discipulus*, from the same root, means "pupil, student, follower," which is where we get the word *disciple*.[XVI]

Discipline develops disciples, and it requires humility and teachability on our part. Consider the following benefits of discipline, growth, and correction that lead us to maturity:

- Training: A pupil is not above his teacher, but everyone, after he has been fully trained, will be like his teacher. (Luke 6:40)
- Teaching: Therefore leaving the elementary teaching about Christ, let us press on to maturity. (Heb 6:1)
- Wisdom: Listen to counsel and accept discipline, that you may be wise the rest of your days. (Prov 19:20)

As we cultivate discipline, consistency, and sound habits, we mature and build a firm foundation that sustains us through internal waves of emotion and external challenges. Spiritual disciplines aren't God's requirement, but they're for our benefit. God has rich treasures in store for us, but we have to take time to pursue Him diligently at all times, not driven by emotion or only when something goes wrong.

As you prepare to fast, consider making time daily for the following practices. This is not an exhaustive study of spiritual disciplines, but an overview of some of the habits I've found most vital to a time of fasting. Some of these may be new to you, or this may simply be a review. We'll talk about scripture, prayer, worship, meditation, and journaling which all go hand in hand and overlap with one another.

Reading the word of God

The absence of vital force in praying can be traced to the absence of a constant supply of God's Word, to repair the water, and renew the life. He who would learn to pray well, must first study God's Word and store it in his memory and thought. —

E.M. Bounds

Americans are exposed to anywhere from 4,000 to 10,000 marketing messages a day.[XVII] That's a load of verbal and visual input to sort through. We need to be sure our minds are refreshed every day with truth that isn't changing and conflicting, and that's why reading the Bible is so vital.

Jesus was the word: "In the beginning was the Word, and the Word was with God, and the Word was God." (John 1:1) It can be difficult to have a relationship with someone you've never physically met, but God reveals Himself to us and speaks to us through His word. It's the primary way we get to know Him.

The Bible describes God's nature. It shows us the rich history of how people have interacted with God, Jesus, and the Holy Spirit. We find the foundational principles for godly living and promises for the future. With the many benefits we receive, we know that "All Scripture is God-breathed and is useful for teaching, rebuking, correcting and training in righteousness, so that the servant of God may be thoroughly equipped for every good work." (2 Tim 3:16–17)

While you may understand the importance of reading the Word, you may struggle with boredom as you read. But rest assured, you can seek help during your studies. Jesus told His disciples that He would send the Holy Spirit to guide and remind them of His teaching (John 16:13). The Holy Spirit also comes to help us, both by revealing what's in the word of God and reminding us of the truth we've read.

While there's no rule that says we have to read through the entire Bible every year, we do need to invest time to study in breadth and depth. We need to read for breadth, covering every book of the Bible, so we understand the entire context. Reading for depth is also important. As you read, pause and consider if you actually connect with what you're reading or if your mind is distracted and you're scanning on autopilot. Take time to not just read over the Word, but to meditate, research, and study. There are many free resources online where you can look up the original meaning of words, read commentaries, or further investigate the scriptures. One of my favorites is blueletterbible.org.

As you read the Bible, remember, "the word of God is alive and active. Sharper than any double-edged sword, it penetrates even to dividing soul and spirit, joints and marrow; it judges the thoughts and attitudes of the heart." (Heb 4:12) The Bible contains timeless truths and principles, and your prayers can also be answered in very specific ways as you read His word! During your time of fasting, you will truly need the word of God as your living bread and daily sustenance.

Prayer

The intercessor lives very close to the heart of God. He has an intimacy with the Lord of creation that few ever know.—Leonard Ravenhill

Whenever you read about fasting in the Bible, prayer is also in the picture. God calls us to connect to Him every day through prayer.

With everything going on in our lives, we desperately need a connection with God every day. The state of the world may seem grim and you may be stressed from the news you hear, but you can take every worry, celebration, and issue that you face directly to God. There is nothing too insignificant or too big. He cares about the smallest detail of your life, and He can also impact the most far-reaching worldwide issue.

The importance of prayer is clear, and while it is a simple concept, it can often feel difficult. It's okay if it is hard for you to know what to say; keep trying without worrying about how the words come out. If your mind wanders when you pray or you have a hard time getting started, try these tips to help you focus:

- Turn on a worship song, inviting God's presence and singing the words out as a prayer.
- Read scripture out loud. The Psalms are especially helpful to get your mind on track.
- Write down your prayers to help you stay focused.

It can also feel difficult if you quickly run out of things to say.

Prayer is a conversation between you and God, which means both talking and listening, so don't be afraid of the pauses—maybe it's His turn to talk. Talk to the Lord like you would your closest friend and be completely honest. You can't hide anything from Him anyway, and when you're alone in prayer, you have no one to impress. Allowing yourself to be brutally and completely honest with God brings immense emotional and spiritual relief. Just look at the Psalms for some raw emotion and real talk.

As you pray, remember the second part of a conversation is to listen. We all want our prayers answered when we want and how we want, but more often than not, God doesn't poof down and wave a magic wand to instantly grant our wishes. But that doesn't mean He's slow in keeping His promises. Imagine where you would be if you got everything you thought you wanted when you were a teenager! During delays and periods of silence, it may be that we are in the sweet spot for revelation.

What to pray for

It's natural to pray for what you want. But the next step is to ask God to reveal what He wants, align your mind with His, and then declare that in prayer. One way to do this is to pray the word of God out loud—over yourself, others, and the world.

Jesus's disciples wanted specific instruction for prayer, and He gave them a guideline in Matthew 6:5–14. He tells them to pray alone with their heavenly Father in a private place. He also gives keys to powerful prayer which could be outlined in the following way:

- Declare God's nature and His greatness, remind yourself who He is as Father and Lord.
- Call out His kingdom amid earthly circumstances, remembering the promises of heaven.
- Give Him control.
- Ask Him for provision. Remember you can depend on Him for every need.
- Confess your sins and forgive others, remembering that we all have sin in our lives and forgiveness is necessary not only for others but also for ourselves.
- Pray for protection from temptation and evil.

A note on this point about confessing sins. We don't like this word, but we can't ignore it. Sin causes separation from God and can be a block in our relationship with Him. We simply have to confess (admit and name) and repent, asking God for forgiveness and turning back to Him. Yet we can easily forget this step as we mature in our faith, and we have the tendency to dismiss or overlook our sins.

As long as we haven't punched someone in the face or stolen something, we gloss over other misdeeds and don't name sin for what it is: a transgression against God that causes separation. Prayer is the time to be transparent with our heavenly Father about everything, including jealousy, pride, bitterness, gossip, or unforgiveness. Although they seem minor and easy to hide, these unaddressed sins ultimately hurt us, block us, and prevent us from moving forward in a healthy, healed, and whole manner.

The good news is, "If we confess our sins, He is faithful and righteous to forgive us our sins and to cleanse us from all unrighteousness." (1 John 1:9) This scripture seals the deal. He will always forgive. Once we confess our sin, we don't have to revisit the matter, berate ourselves, or do penance. He forgives us and He makes all things new.

Summary

Intercessory prayer is essential, so we should bring our requests to Him. Prayer also includes praising God, thanking Him, and declaring His goodness. Prayer involves confessing our sins, working through forgiveness, and engaging in spiritual warfare. And most importantly, prayer involves listening and allowing God to speak to us. As you fast, dive into your prayer life like never before, remembering that throughout history, prayer and fasting have gone hand in hand.

Worship

Worship is a Spiritual Discipline insofar as it is both an end and a means . . . the more truly we worship God, the more we become like Him.—Donald Whitney

Worship is about exalting God with our whole heart in every situation. Worship is both reactive and proactive. After all, worshiping God is a natural reaction to who He is and what He has done. Reflecting on His goodness and nature naturally inspires worship, and as we worship, we invite the presence of God. There's no formula to experiencing His powerful, holy presence, but God has given us the directive to seek Him with our whole heart.

This charge is where the proactive part comes into play. The Bible is clear that both public and private worship are important. Hebrews 10:25 calls us to come together, and the Bible is full of corporate worship and prayer, particularly throughout the book of Acts and New Testament epistles. Be sure to find a church you can commit to regularly attend; corporate worship, along with teaching and community, are a vital part of your spiritual life.

We are also called to worship God privately. Quiet time and devotionals will feel dry and rote if we don't create a sacred space for the Lord and invite His presence. God calls us to seek Him directly; He wants to meet us one on one. C.S. Lewis said, "Only in the act of praise and worship can a person learn to believe in the goodness and greatness of God."

Music

The sound and experience of music touch our soul and spirit in a unique way. Music is a means of praising and worshiping God, but worship encompasses more than singing and doesn't require musical skills or abilities.

The Bible has many examples of singing as a form of worship. Psalms is an entire book of hymns. In the New Testament, Jesus and

His disciples sang after the Last Supper (Matt 26:30). When Paul and Silas were in prison, they were freed as they were "praying and singing hymns." (Acts 16:25) Ephesians 5:19 instructs the church to speak to one another in psalms and hymns and spiritual songs. We're missing out if we only sing to God while we're in church. Take music with you everywhere you go to saturate your environment and your heart.

Putting God first

Although we frequently call the singing portion of Sunday service "worship," the practice of worshiping God extends beyond music. The Hebrew word for worship is shachah which literally means to bow down, prostrate oneself, and reverence.[XVIII] The Old Testament has a lot to say about the importance of choosing whom (or what) to worship.

God's people struggled with this question throughout history, vacillating between loyalty to Yahweh and worshiping pagan gods and idols. Sometimes the Israelites presented their sacrifices and offerings to God, but other times they drifted, giving offerings to pagan idols and worshiping at their altars.

One of the most infamous examples of misguided worship is the golden calf in Exodus 32. While Moses was on the mountain communing with God for an extended period, the people convinced his brother, Aaron, to melt gold and create a calf.

They built an altar, offered sacrifices to this golden idol, and were singing and dancing in the camp. You can read more, but this did not end well when Moses came down. He thoroughly addressed this situation and established boundaries as he presented the law.

You probably haven't set up a statue in your backyard, but an idol is not necessarily a physical object. Is there something in your life you value too highly and look to as your source of power, control, and provision above God? This becomes a form of worship as we give excessive worth to these things. We can idolize people, personal qualities, material things, or even ourselves.

We have the same tendency as the Israelites. It can be easier to idolize and put our faith in something tangible than to trust an invisible God. As we make worship a purposeful daily practice, we remind our hearts and souls to put God first, so worship him wholeheartedly as you fast.

Summary

Worship is about making God first in your life in every way, always remembering He is worthy of our honor and praise. Bowing down requires humility and admitting you don't have all the answers. As you worship, you place yourself in a posture of dependence on God for wisdom, provision, and protection.

Worship can be full of emotion but isn't driven by emotion. It may include music but extends beyond music. Worship is essential in these times, and Jesus was very clear on this subject: "An hour is coming, and now is, when the true worshipers will worship the Father in spirit and truth; for such people the Father seeks to be His worshipers." (John 4:23) Let your time of fasting be filled with joyful worship.

Meditation

May the words of my mouth and the meditation of my heart be acceptable in your sight, Lord, my rock and my Redeemer. —Ps 19:14

The practice of meditation dates back to 1500 BCE and spans many cultures and religious practices. Meditation can be challenging to define because the label is used for a range of activities, from informal practices like a few moments of silence and deep breathing to a regimented religious practice.[XIX] You can easily find numerous meditation apps, podcasts, and blog articles on the subject of meditation.

Even though it's mentioned throughout the Bible, it can be difficult to find meditation resources in churches. We can skirt the issue of meditation because of concerns that it's too entangled with other religions, ideas, and practices that don't line up with the Bible. But the solution is to study what the word of God says, not avoid the topic altogether.

It's also worth considering the mental and physical benefits of deep breathing, mindfulness, and focused concentration—all practices that accompany most forms of meditation. According to the National Institute of Mental Health, over 30 percent of adult Americans experience an anxiety disorder at some point in their lifetime.[XX] People are seeking solutions to decrease stress and restore mental and emotional well-being.

Proponents of meditation claim that regular practice decreases stress and anxiety and improves sleep and emotional health. Research has shown that meditation has positive health effects, although the results of scientific studies are not always consistent because the definition of meditation varies so widely.[XXI]

Biblical meditation

Biblical meditation, by definition, is reflection and musing and also means to mutter or utter. This form of meditation is not just a vacuum of emptiness but active thinking, concentration, musing and study, prayer, and purposeful speaking.[XXII] Our resting mental state is not a flat line, our brains are constantly working. In our loud and fast-paced world, moments of stillness and reflection can restore and replenish our souls like nothing else.

In Luke 6:45, Jesus said the mouth speaks from that which fills the heart. As thoughts become words, they powerfully shape our attitudes, actions, and reality. This is why it's so vital to meditate on the right things! Joshua is instructed to meditate on the law day and night, in order to do all that is written in it (Josh 1:8).

Isaac went out to meditate in the field in the evening in Genesis 24:63. When Peter went up on the housetop at the sixth hour to meditate and pray, he received his vision about ministry to the Gentiles (Acts 10:9). As we've already seen, Daniel made a regular practice of prayer three times a day.

Prayer, meditation, and Bible reading go hand in hand. You can choose a scripture to reflect on and repeat. You can think about it, repeat it out loud, and write it down. You can emphasize a different word of the passage each time, pausing as long as needed. We tend to read for quantity, but meditation involves taking one truth and examining every dimension, allowing it to soak in our mind and heart.

Biblical meditation involves concentrating on scripture and the nature of God. When your mind wanders, which it will naturally do, you acknowledge those thoughts without judgment but then dismiss them and bring your attention back, time and again.

How to meditate

So how do you meditate practically? You don't have to sit on the floor with your legs crossed and a candle burning, but a quiet environment and sitting up straight in a comfortable position are ideal. Even with the right environment, quiet concentration is a habit that takes time to develop. Setting aside a regular time to meditate is key to developing a consistent habit. You may initially only be able to stay still for a few minutes, but find a baseline and gradually add to it.

Meditation and deep breathing complement each other. Slowing and deepening your breath causes a physiological response that calms the body and mind.[XXIII] Take a few minutes to concentrate on your breathing as you begin, and when your thoughts drift off track, taking deep breaths and focusing on the inhale and exhale can help you re-center and focus. You can also do a body scan, focusing on one muscle group or body part at a time and purposefully letting go of tension and relaxing.

Even if meditation feels awkward initially, give yourself a few moments daily to connect your mind, heart, and body in stillness and reflective concentration.

Journaling

Write the vision and make it plain on tablets, that he may run who reads it.—
Hab 2:2 NKJV

When I was little, I loved diaries with little padlocks and tiny keys. It was comforting to write down my secrets and lock them up safe. Ironically, even if someone had found the key, I don't think I ever had any profound or shocking secrets. But there is a special comfort in knowing you can be honest and fully transparent, airing all your thoughts and feelings.

I still need that private space for internal reflection and processing. I have a bookshelf with several dozen journals kept over the years. Some are workbooks from Bible studies or sermon notes. Others are personal journals with thoughts and reflections. I've bought formatted prayer journals, gratitude journals, and daily diaries. Although I'm not perfectly consistent, journaling has become an essential habit for me.

Writing can be reflective, a form of active prayer, or visionary for the future. When you fast, you're going to have unique experiences and revelations that you'll want to record for future reference. You may also have emotions and memories that surface during this time, and need a dedicated safe place to process them.

As Christians, we usually know the right answers to our petty worries and stresses: we should have faith, trust God, and pray about it. So sometimes we bury our less lovely thoughts and feelings because we know better . . . but that doesn't necessarily mean they're gone. Those stuffed thoughts and feelings can simmer and explode at the wrong time, or cause a root of bitterness that's poisonous long-term.

Although you know certain anxieties aren't valid and everything will work out, these mental lurkers can scratch at the back of your mind until you process them and get them out in the open. Moving things from dark to light brings clarity and leads to resolution. Journaling can be a way to process, as writing helps you express your feelings and identify underlying tension and the root cause of issues you're dealing with.

The Bible says it's important to keep records. God instructs the Israelites to record stories and pass them on to future generations to remind them of what God has done. He even told the Israelites to write the statutes on the doorposts and gates as a reminder (Deut 6:9).

You may write down things you'd rather not publish on the Internet, but keeping a record of struggles, revelations, triumphs, and answered prayers will be a future encouragement to yourself and others. I'm amazed when I look back at my journals. God has taught me incredible lessons over the years, but I might remember less than 1 percent of it unless I write it down!

What and how to journal

Methods of journaling are entirely a personal preference. You can use an app or computer, but I prefer to write by hand. I think there's power in the physical, tangible act of writing. My most recent practice has been to wake up every morning and write in a plain journal:

1. Three things I'm grateful for

2. One to three things causing me stress

3. My top memory (from the day before)

4. What Bible verses I am reading

5. My prayers

6. Any dreams I remember

7. Any additional thoughts and feelings to process

8. My intention and goals for the day

This sounds like a lot, but it's usually just one or two pages. If you'd like to download a sample of this daily journal, you can find it at danielfastjourney.com/bookresources. The first point is especially important. Practicing gratitude and training yourself to focus on the good will transform your mindset. And think about it, if you write three things you're grateful for every day, you'll record over a thousand blessings a year.

I already mentioned the importance of writing down stresses (better out than in). In the Psalms, you'll find records of David lamenting over his issues, but he always returned his focus to God by the end. As he works through difficulties then shifts his perspective, the Psalms end on a triumphal note. We can work through that same cycle when we journal.

Even if you don't write in a journal every day, it's important to keep one while you fast. As you seek God, He will speak to you. Make sure you write down your prayers, revelations from the Lord, and everything that happens during this time.

Your Journey

Fasting is a special time of growth, and it's all the richer when we make time for regular spiritual disciplines like those mentioned in this chapter and others that we didn't have time to talk about here. Note that this isn't an exhaustive list and examination of spiritual disciplines.

You may feel called to give, serve, or grow closer to God in another way during this time. Whatever you do, keep a record of all your experiences and continue to commit to simple habits that strengthen your relationship with God as you invest in spending time with Him.

Chapter 5 Reflections

• Which of the spiritual disciplines mentioned in this chapter are most appealing or natural for you to practice?

• Are there any that are not part of your regular routine but you'd like to practice while fasting?

• Do you consider yourself a disciplined person? What role do you think discipline plays for you personally as you continue to mature in your faith?

Chapter 6

Survey Your Environment: Planning to Fast

But you, when you fast, anoint your head and wash your face so that your fasting will not be noticed by men, but by your Father who is in secret; and your Father who sees what is done in secret will reward you. —Matt 6:17–18

The purpose of fasting is to loosen to some degree the ties which bind us to the world of material things and our surroundings as a whole, in order that we may concentrate all our spiritual powers upon the unseen and eternal things.
—Ole Hallesby

Fasting was an abstract concept for me growing up. I had heard about it but didn't know anyone who actually fasted until I was in my mid-twenties. When I first heard pastors talk about fasting together as a church community, I felt both excited and terrified.

While I was intrigued by the idea of strengthening my faith, drawing closer to God, and gaining clarity and direction through prayer and fasting, I was terrified because I love to eat, and I despise being hungry.

I avoided the side effects of hunger at all costs, unable to tolerate the gnawing stomach and lightheadedness that resulted from delaying a meal. They invented the word *hangry* for a reason because being too hungry eventually turns you into a rage monster!

And I thought if I did fast, I would be doomed to overeat at the next meal and my metabolism would slow down. After all, the popular diet advice at that time recommended that you eat small meals every few hours to maintain a stable metabolism. Essentially, I was used to eating all day long, so my first experience fasting was a shock to my system.

My first fast, where I consumed only liquids, lasted for three days. My body was unaccustomed to extended breaks from eating, so I was acutely aware of my hunger and its physical side effects. On the second day, I couldn't concentrate on anything. I was fixated on the clock, every second ticking by in slow motion. I crawled to the finish line on the evening of the third day and had a lot to chew on following this experience (pun intended).

Looking back, nothing specific resulted from that first fast in terms of answered prayers or revelations. I didn't see angels or have a groundbreaking insight into my childhood. God didn't speak to me in an audible voice. Honestly, I was mostly fixated on my physical discomfort, and I was beyond relieved when it was over.

But a seed had been planted. The greatest breakthrough from my first fasting experience was a simple realization: I can do this. As the momentary discomfort passed, the internal resolve remained.

As I began fasting more regularly, my body adapted from a physical standpoint. This was true not just for liquid-only fasts, but also when doing Daniel Fasts. Over time, I had fewer and milder side effects, so I was less preoccupied with my state of hunger and what I was eating, and more focused on the spiritual aspect of fasting.

Some of the greatest breakthroughs of my life have come during times of fasting. These revelations may not seem earth-shattering to others, but they mean the world to me personally. For example, one year I was at a morning prayer service during a period of fasting. I had a very clear impression of the Lord saying to me, "You can't forgive yourself for things and move on because you still feel like you're supposed to do penance every time." This was in reference to my religious upbringing and the feeling I had retained that something had to be "done" or "paid for" in order to truly move on past my sins and mistakes. On that day, the Lord made it so clear to me that when I confessed my sins, I was forgiven completely and could freely move forward. There was nothing left for me to do, His love and grace are truly enough.

When you slow down and pay attention, the Lord has a way of bringing up specific memories or highlighting small details in your day that are significant. Over time, fasting uncovered false beliefs I had about food, control, and my faith.

God will always have more to reveal to you. Your relationship with Him can continually grow in depth and intimacy. While fasting may never become a comfortable experience, it will become something you look forward to, knowing the benefits to come.

Getting Started

You can spend a lot of time debating whether you should fast, how you should fast, and when you should fast. But the most important step is the first one: just start. Give up a meal. Fast for one day. See what happens!

Once you have personal experience, you no longer have to rely on other peoples' stories. You'll know for yourself because you walked through it and now have your own testimony to share. Jesus didn't try to sell people on His ministry and discipleship program. He gave a simple directive: "Come and see." (John 1:39, 1:46, 4:29) We have an open invitation to come and fast and then see what happens.

Whether this is your first time or your hundredth time fasting, don't take for granted that you know what to expect. Take time to prepare your spirit, soul, and body. Be sure to pray and ask God, *What does fasting look like for me this time?*

You may be anxious to jump into the food lists and figure out what to eat and avoid. We'll cover that in the next section, but fasting is as much about *how* to eat as it is *what* to eat. Before getting started, there are some details of preparing your body and environment to cover.

When to Fast

A physical and spiritual reset is a great way to start a new season. For this reason, many churches have a corporate time of prayer and fasting at the beginning of the year. It's an opportunity to draw closer to God and seek His direction for the future. Like many others, I start each year with some form of fasting in January.

I love a fresh start. I am quickly bored by routine and look forward to new projects, goals, and adventures. But I have learned an important lesson over the years: pause and pray before you plan. I am prone to take on too many things and run off full speed in a million directions. I'm overwhelmed with the number of things to do before I've even verified if they are the *right* things to be doing.

This happens when we start with goals instead of starting with God. Take time to listen before you start talking and pray before you start planning. There is no rule about how many days you should fast. The Bible references people fasting for a day, three days, ten days, twenty-one days, and forty days, but you don't have to pick one of these exact intervals.

The heart of this book is to make fasting accessible to everyone so it can be a regular part of your worship and devotional life. You can plan times of fasting, whether that's annually or even monthly, and also fast when issues arise or you have specific prayers. Fasting isn't restricted to the month of January or the season of Lent.

Planning ahead doesn't make you less spiritual. God was very specific in how He instructed Noah to build the ark and Moses to establish the law. He told Joshua to march around Jericho one time for six days, then seven times the seventh day. He gave others instructions for how to travel, how to prepare for battles, and the list goes on.

Be intentional as you plan to fast. Look at your calendar for windows of time you're less likely to be derailed by external commitments and potential distractions and plan to fast then. It's not about finding the time that will be easiest for you, but ensuring you'll have enough room in your schedule to spend the most time possible with the Lord. But know that it's possible God could call you to fast during a holiday, vacation, or period of extreme busyness at work, and if He does, He will also give you the grace and resources you need.

Time is a precious commodity. When you are on a Daniel Fast, you will need time to prepare food and cook meals. Many people underestimate this commitment when they begin fasting so make sure you plan with this factor in mind. In addition, as we've said before, fasting is about more than eating. As part of your spiritual rhythm, you want to be able to focus wholeheartedly on God when you fast and have time to pray, read your Bible, and invest in your spiritual life.

Who Needs to Know

Jesus commented that when you fast, you should anoint your head and wash your face so your fasting will not be noticed by men but by your Father who is in secret (Matt 6:17–18). He's reminding

His followers that you don't need to act like a miserable martyr when you fast; it's ultimately between you and God.

Jesus wasn't necessarily commanding us to keep secrets. His point was not to make a spectacle of yourself or fast with superficial motives that highlight your performance and seek the attention and approval of other people. Whatever people might say and think about your fasting, the ultimate reward comes from God.

You don't have to be secretive around people you're close to; just be humble. Your family probably needs to know what you're doing so they can support you. You may even have to explain to your co-workers why you decline every lunch date for a week. This can be a unique opportunity to share your faith. Although some people aren't open to hearing about church services or Bible study, there's natural curiosity around spiritual disciplines like fasting.

If you're the primary cook and grocery shopper in your household, think through how your fast affects meal planning. Everyone in your household may not be fasting alongside you. This is definitely the case if you have children, elderly family members, or anyone whose health would be compromised by fasting.

However, preparing two sets of meals is extra work and requires advance planning, so consider some of the following possibilities:

- Can you make ahead and freeze meals for your kids?
- Will your family have takeout or delivery more frequently for this period of time?
- Can family members help to make their own dinners?

• Have you created a meal plan for them and stocked the foods they need?

Fasting can be a great teaching moment for your children. Limiting food intake is not safe or appropriate for them because adequate nutrition is essential for their growing bodies. But your children may decide to give up junk food or take a break from video games. They can join in spirit and focus on abstaining from unhealthy habits and drawing closer to God through a special time of prayer.

This shouldn't be forced on them. If it's not their idea and personal conviction, then they won't have the heart for it. As a teaching moment, you can explain what fasting is and why you've decided to do it. Then, if they show interest, let them participate in brainstorming some ideas of how they could take special time to focus on their relationship with God. Most importantly, you can pray together during this time and share your fasting journey with them along the way.

Before You Fast

Here's a word of caution about your transition as you prepare to fast. Have you ever experienced a bumpy airplane during takeoff or landing? Runways are engineered to provide ample room for a smooth transition into the air and then back to the ground. But sometimes you have a scary landing.

You know the kind: the plane bangs down on the runway going full speed, and your head snaps forward. There's a loud whirring of wheels and a moment of panic as you question whether the pilot will actually be able to stop in time.

Fortunately, the brakes on my planes have always worked. But I would rather not experience this kind of racing heart and sweaty palm landing; I prefer the smooth landing.

In the same way, your body typically does not respond well to abrupt changes. Not only is it uncomfortable, but in the worst case, it can also be dangerous. Taking a short amount of time to transition into your fast will help you avoid unwanted physical side effects.

And when you're not distracted by physical side effects, your spiritual focus while fasting will be stronger. Side effects during fasting can include fatigue, headaches (especially from caffeine withdrawal), mental fog, lethargy, and obviously, hunger pains and cravings. On a Daniel Fast, you can also experience a variety of digestive issues, including cramping and frequent trips to the bathroom, if you too rapidly increase the amount of fiber in your diet.

There's a significant difference between my regular diet and the Daniel Fast. Although we eat an overall healthy diet in our home, we consume many things each week that would not be part of a Daniel Fast. We typically eat out or pick up food once or twice a week. There's usually a birthday party, holiday, or other social occasions where desserts and special treats are available. And most significant for me personally, I have a minimum of one cup of coffee with cream a day (and rarely restrict myself to the minimum). Even with my prior experience with the Daniel Fast, I am mindful of preparing my body, household, and kitchen before I fast because when I don't, it's never a good experience.

Health and food consumption

Before you fast, it's critical to assess your health from a medical standpoint. Consult a doctor if you have any pre-existing health conditions, take any medication, or are pregnant or nursing. Be sure you have proper clearance for any major change to your eating plan. Please don't skip this step!

Next, honestly assess your current diet and eating patterns. Simply write down what you would eat in a typical week. Are you eating meat at every meal? Do you consume soft drinks throughout the day? Do you get fast food or go out to restaurants several times a week?

All these habits have to shift when you're fasting. A "cold turkey" stop is tough. When you quit consuming processed foods, your body needs time to process and eliminate artificial preservatives and unhealthy substances. You have to work through side effects and adjust to a different dietary composition.

When you replace junk foods with more nutrient-dense foods, your body will have the nutritional support it needs. And this will help you recalibrate and prepare for fasting. At least five to seven days before your Daniel Fast, start to gradually adjust your diet according to the following:

Gradually Decrease	Gradually Increase
• Meat to one meal per day • Dairy products • Bread and baked goods • Sugar • Processed foods • Beverages other than water • Alcohol	• Vegetables and fruits • Beans and legumes to 1 serving a day • Whole grains • Fiber • Water: drink 64 oz. a day minimum, or preferably 2.7 liters for women and 3.7 liters for men daily • Sleep 7–9 hours a night

Sleep

Our sleeping habits have a tremendous impact on our well-being. If we sleep the recommended seven to nine hours a night, we're spending a third of our lives in bed. Although we're unconscious during sleep, a lot is going on in our bodies and brains, so we need to make sure we have quantity and quality time sleeping.

Sleep is the body's best source of natural health and energy, but too often we cut corners and power through our days with caffeine and sugar. When you fast, you're stripping away these artificial energy boosts, and it will be more essential than ever to get enough rest.

As noted in *The Sleep Revolution*, sleep is not empty time. It's a period of rich neurological activity, including memory consolidation, brain and neurochemical cleansing, renewal, and cognitive mainte-nance. Physically, your body is able to repair and grow as you sleep. Sleep even helps to enhance your immune system.[XXIV]

Also, remember that in the Bible, God frequently spoke to peo-ple through dreams or during the night. You may not remember your dreams easily, but you can start by writing down the brief moments and images you do recall when you wake up.

If you have a difficult time falling and staying asleep, here are a few basic tips to improve your sleep life:

- Go to sleep and wake up at the same time each day.
- Get natural light each day, preferably in the morning, to help regulate your circadian rhythms.
- Exercise daily, but avoid vigorous exercise too close to bedtime.
- Develop a relaxing nighttime ritual and be sure to avoid screens at least an hour or two before bedtime.
- Make sure your bedroom is a relaxing environment: keep it dark, maintain a comfortable temperature, and avoid doing work or other activities in bed.[XXV]

For the many spiritual, mental, and physical health benefits, be sure to prioritize sleep as an opportunity to restore yourself not only when you fast, but always.

Exercise

What does your current exercise routine look like? This is your starting point for physical activity during your Daniel Fast. If you don't have any health conditions and currently have an intense work-out regimen, there's evidence you can maintain your routine while fasting with no adverse effects. But it would be wise to modify activity for the first few days as your body adjusts to fasting.

If you're not currently exercising regularly and consistently, this isn't the time to start an intense workout plan. Thirty minutes a day of moderate activity, such as biking, walking, or strength training, is sufficient to gain the many benefits of exercise.

Think of activities that will enhance your fasting experience, not distract from it. A two-hour gym outing will eat up a lot of your time and could be energy depleting, but a morning walk can be an opportunity for contemplation and prayer, and easier to incorporate into your routine.

Physical activity boosts your mood, aids digestion, and helps you sleep better. A well-rounded routine includes exercises for cardiorespiratory endurance, muscular strength training, and flexibility.

As you're strengthening your spirit during this time, you also have the opportunity to focus on your total well-being and take better care of your body by establishing long-lasting healthy habits, like making time for a good night's sleep and daily physical activity.

A "Media Fast"

One last thing to think about as you prepare to fast is what your approach to media will be during your fast. This includes social media, TV, books, and magazines. I have heard people mention a "media fast" as one of several options for fasting, meaning you take a break or abstain from specific kinds of media for a period of time. While this is a great idea, fasting defined in the Bible means going without food. Although not necessarily a fast by itself, there are many benefits to restricting your intake of social media, TV, etc. while fasting.

The media is constantly bombarding you with propositions to improve literally everything about your life. Lose weight, have more energy, get in shape, buy the right car or the right house, be a better parent, and the list goes on forever.

When you have too much input and not enough time for reflection and implementation, you can become confused about what to do or discouraged that you're not living up to expectations. The worst part is, these usually aren't realistic or God-centered expectations.

Social media in particular causes you to compare yourself to peoples' filtered lives, and causes you to qualify your worth based on the likes and responses from others. None of this is beneficial, especially when you're on a fast and trying to detach from the world and focus on your spiritual life.

I recommend trying to cut down on all media sources any time you fast. This will give you fewer distractions, and more time to focus on God. Fasting is the perfect time to sit back in reflection and examine where you took a wrong turn, believed a lie, or developed a false expectation because of cultural messages and pressure.

When I get stressed and overwhelmed, I frequently ask myself,

"Why am I even doing this?" When I pause and reflect, usually the driving forces behind my efforts are fear, competition, comparison, or concern about others' opinions. None of these things align with God's will but are in plentiful supply from the media.

God does not give us a spirit of fear; He wants us to trust in Him and seek His approval, not popular opinion. For that reason, the more we limit our intake and focus on consuming godly wisdom, the better off we'll be.

Prepare for Landing

An extra note before you get too far in the process: Commit to ending well. When you're nearing the end of your fast, you'll be salivating over the meals and snacks you've missed. However, you can't give in to the temptation to stuff yourself with all those foods the moment your fast is over.

After you've adjusted to eating a clean diet, eating too much can literally make you sick. So go slowly. Gradually reintroduce food items you've been abstaining from and see how your body reacts. Also, consider the positive changes that resulted from your new eating habits. Although it's incredibly easy to immediately slip back into old eating habits, you could benefit from incorporating elements of the Daniel Fast year-round.

Don't be all or nothing when it comes to your habits. Whether it's how you're eating or the time you're spending with God, let each time you fast be a step towards building a transformed lifestyle with a healthier spirit, soul, and body.

Your Journey

Maybe you've never fasted before or perhaps you already fast regularly. Either way, each experience of fasting is special. You're in a unique position physically, mentally, and spiritually. Don't take anything for granted, but be intentional in prayer and planning every time.

What do you need to plan, who do you need to talk to? How can you adjust your sleep and exercise schedule? Pray about when to start and the length of your fast. Also, consider how you will transition into and out of your fast.

Chapter 6 Reflections

• When are the best times during the year for you to fast? Do you have any significant moments coming up that would prompt you to fast?

• How will you prepare physically leading up to your fast? What changes do you need to make in sleep, exercise, and eating?

• How will you cut down on social media, TV, etc. during this time? Is this an area where you struggle with balance?

PART FOUR
REVITALIZE YOUR BODY

Chapter 7

Gather Your Supplies: What to Eat on a Daniel Fast

Please test your servants for ten days, and let us be given some vegetables to eat and water to drink.—Dan 1:12

Fasting is not an end in itself; it is a means by which we can worship the Lord and submit ourselves in humility to Him. We don't make God love us any more than He already does if we fast, or if we fast longer . . . [Fasting] invites God into the problem. Then in the strength of God, victory is possible.—Elmer L. Towns

Can you imagine the effort it took to prepare a meal 2,000 years ago? It looks vastly different than how we operate today. We can walk into a grocery store and find rows upon rows of ready-to-eat snacks, neatly packaged meats, and fresh produce shipped in from around the world. Simply heat in the microwave and dinner can be ready in five minutes or less.

With our advancements in efficiency, our society produces a higher volume of food and figures out ways to distribute and preserve it for years. But as a major drawback to this, the nutritional value in our food decreases the more it is processed.

While the loss of nutritional value is bad enough, our food also contains unhealthy additives. Food manufacturers have made food more desirable by adding salt, sugar, and other preservatives to create the most attractive colors, textures, and flavors. These foods are usually calorie-dense, but nutrient-poor. This excess energy (i.e., calories) will likely be stored as fat, while these foods provide little of the essential nutrients your body needs to thrive.

In the past, people's options were limited to what grew naturally in their environment. And the effort of growing, harvesting, and preparing food consumed their lives. For example, bread was a daily staple of ancient diets, but it took an estimated three hours to grind enough flour to feed five to six people. After producing the flour, they then spent additional time preparing the bread, letting it rise, and baking it.[xxvi] Preparing the daily bread was literally an all-day endeavor.

Mindset for a Daniel Fast

If we compare our diet and eating habits to those in ancient times, we are clearly starting from a very different baseline when it comes to fasting. It's not so simple for us to just eat like Daniel did during his ten days because we don't have a list of precisely what he ate and our food supply is vastly different. As a result, we have done some modern interpretation of what it looks like to eat during a Daniel Fast.

Because of the nature of the typical American diet, I am purposely spending some time on this issue before we get into food lists. It's important for you to understand that any step you make to fast, and specifically for a Daniel Fast, is a huge leap for your physical and spiritual health, even if it doesn't look exactly like what someone else is doing.

Here are some facts to consider. Over 36 percent of Americans consume fast food daily. Not every week, we're talking about every day.[XXVII] The average US consumption of meat and animal products is higher than recommended in the *Dietary Guidelines* and has increased over the past forty years. Additionally, a study in 2017 reported that only one in ten American adults is eating the recommended number of servings of fruits and vegetables each day.[XXVIII]

With a Daniel Fast, you'll abstain from certain food groups including meat, eggs, and dairy and eat more fruits and vegetables. This is a radical shift from the Standard American Diet many of us are consuming. Along with the standard protocol for a Daniel Fast meal plan, you need to consider the following: Will you consume foods that are plant-based but packaged or minimally processed?

A variety of items fall into this category. A package of almonds may seem safe, but you have to read the ingredients carefully to check whether they are raw or have added salt, sugar, seasonings, and preservatives. Even if foods contain all-natural, plant-based ingredients, some people would propose that all packaged foods should be eliminated on a Daniel Fast, and certain ingredients such as soy or gluten should be completely avoided when you're fasting.

People have said that a Daniel Fast is basically a vegan diet, but there are some unique differences. Although a vegan diet doesn't include animal products, it still allows baked goods, packaged snacks, and processed foods. Vegan meal plans might also include alcohol, caffeine, and desserts that wouldn't be included on a Daniel Fast. So while vegan cookbooks are extremely helpful when you're on a Daniel Fast, just double-check the recipe ingredients in advance to ensure they are Daniel Fast friendly.

Fresh produce and Daniel Fast meals can be tasty, but it will be different from what you are used to. You won't find any dessert recipes in this book, and a Daniel Fast isn't a time to indulge. Although you can (and should) enjoy your food, you're not eating in response to cravings. You're eating to live, not living to eat.

Differing viewpoints

After posting my original Daniel Fast meal plan on my blog, I received an e-mail from a lady who seemed very irate because I had foods that she felt should not be included on a Daniel Fast, the main offense being peanut butter. In her e-mail, she implored me to repent and not grieve the Holy Spirit any longer.

My first reaction was panic. What had I done? What damage had I caused? Should I delete everything? My next reaction was confusion: Who decides what can and cannot be on the food list?

I was certain steak and wine were out of the picture on a Daniel Fast. Beyond that, I thought anything under the umbrella of plant-based foods could be included. Because peanut butter came from nuts and didn't contain any animal products, I assumed it was acceptable. But I learned another perspective and opinion, which is that the Daniel Fast should not include any processed foods whatsoever.

I am thankful for this criticism because it caused me to pray, research, dig into the Bible, and clarify my convictions for fasting. I encourage you to do the same and be intentional. Exactly what you decide to eat or not eat when you fast is between you and God; it doesn't have to look identical to someone else's plan or be exactly the same every time you fast.

I take part in a Daniel Fast several times a year. Sometimes I include peanut butter and almond milk, and sometimes I don't. And when I do, I choose the least processed version available, such as unsweetened, unflavored milk substitutes and peanut butter that's ground fresh in-store (even major grocery stores often have this grinder in the bulk health food section that uses only peanuts).

But honestly, it's less important to argue about whether you can eat peanut butter, canned soup, and Triscuits on a Daniel Fast and more critical that you get the larger picture and core principles in place.

What Would Daniel Eat?

Remember the motivation for Daniel's request in chapter one. He was primarily concerned with not defiling himself with the king's food and wine. Daniel asked to be tested for ten days by eating only vegetables and drinking only water (Dan 1:12).

Even though meat and animal products were part of a standard Jewish diet, they had to be prepared in a specific way following the law. So Daniel wasn't willing to eat food that had been defiled in its preparation or was part of idol worship because this would violate the Jewish law.

The King James Version says Daniel asked for *pulse* to eat. The definition of pulse means herbs or vegetable food in general or seed used for food. For a Daniel Fast, this has been commonly interpreted to include any type of whole grains, beans, legumes, seeds, and nuts.

The Bible doesn't specify exactly what foods Daniel ate during those ten days, but we have an idea of what might have been eaten based on other biblical passages and additional archeological research. (Although meat was part of the ancient Jewish diet, the discussion in this chapter includes only plant-based foods for the purpose of discussing the Daniel Fast.)

Deuteronomy 8:7–8 talks about the foods to be found in the promised land, which include wheat, barley, vines (grapes), fig trees, pomegranates, olive oil, and honey. These foods have been referred to as the *seven species* of ancient Israel.[xxx]

When grain is mentioned in the Bible, it's typically a reference to wheat or barley. These grains were commonly consumed in one of the following ways: ground into flour and baked into bread, parched or toasted (as seen in Lev 2:14, Ruth 2:14, and 1 Sam 17:17), or boiled in water to make gruel or porridge.[XXXI]

Other foods mentioned in the Bible, or determined to have been present in ancient times by archaeologists, include the following:

SAMPLE OF FOODS EATEN IN ANCIENT TIMES	
• Dates	• Melons
• Figs	• Leeks, onions, and garlic
• Pomegranates	• Wild grasses/lettuces and
• Carobs (a tree that produces fruit and honey)	herbs
• Citron	• Lentils
• Walnuts	• Chickpeas
• Almonds	• Broad bean or fava bean
• Peaches	• Barley
• Apples	• Millet
• Plums	• Wheat/spelt
• Apricots	• Herbs and spices including
• Capers	aloes, anise/fennel, bay
• Cucumbers/zucchini	leaves, cinnamon, cumin,
	coriander, mint, mustard,
	saffron, sage, salt

What to Eat on Your Daniel Fast

If you compare the list above with your everyday diet, I would imagine you have very little overlap. The typical western diet contains plentiful amounts of animal products, processed grains, and beverages containing calories, sugar, and caffeine.

So now we move into exactly what to eat, which is probably the reason you're reading this book. The remainder of this chapter includes a few helpful references. First are lists of foods to include and exclude on a Daniel Fast. This is the baseline framework for what to eat. Next, there are two filters for making decisions about other food items not mentioned here. You can also find printable versions of the food lists in this chapter at danielfastjourney.com/bookresources.

FOODS TO INCLUDE ON A DANIEL FAST

Fruits and Vegetables*	Whole Grains
• Apples	• Amaranth
• Avocado	• Barley
• Bananas	• Bulgur
• Berries	• Brown Rice
• Dates	• Farro
• Figs	• Grits/Polenta
• Kiwi	• Millet
• Grapes	• Oats
• Lemons and Limes	• Quinoa
• Mango	

- Melons
- Oranges and Grapefruit
- Pears
- Peaches, Plums, Nectarines
- Pineapples
- Pomegranates
- Artichoke
- Asparagus
- Beets
- Bell Peppers
- Bok Choy
- Broccoli
- Brussels Sprouts
- Cabbage
- Carrot
- Cauliflower
- Celery
- Corn
- Cucumber
- Edamame
- Eggplant
- Ginger
- Green Beans
- Kale
- Lettuce and Greens (arugula, endive, swiss chard,etc.)
- Mushrooms
- Okra
- Onions and Garlic
- Peas, Snap Peas
- Potatoes and Sweet Potatoes
- Spinach
- Squash and Zucchini
- Tomatoes
- Turnips

Legumes
- Beans, all types including black, kidney, pinto, white
- Black-eyed peas
- Chickpeas/garbanzo beans
- Lentils
- Peas
- Soybeans

Nuts and Seeds
- Almonds
- Brazil Nuts
- Cashews
- Hazelnuts
- Peanuts
- Pecans
- Pistachios
- Walnuts
- Pumpkin Seeds
- Sesame Seeds
- Sunflower Seeds

Other
- Fresh or dried herbs and spices
- Olives
- Pure plant-based oils (olive,
- grapeseed, sesame)
- Sea salt or Himalayan salt

All fruits and vegetables are included on the Daniel Fast: fresh, frozen, canned, or dried (check ingredient labels).

FOODS TO ABSTAIN FROM ON A DANIEL FAST

Animal Products

Dairy
- Butter or Margarine
- Cheese (all types)
- Cream or Half & Half
- Cream cheese
- Cottage cheese/curds
- Custard
- Ice cream/frozen yogurt
- Milk
- Pudding
- Sour cream
- Yogurt

Eggs

Meat
- Beef
- Bison
- Chicken
- Lamb
- Pork
- Bacon, salami, cured meats
- Turkey

Seafood
- Crab
- Lobster
- Fish (all types)
- Shrimp
- Other shellfish
  (Clams, Mussels, Oysters)

Beverages other than water or herbal tea
- Alcohol
- Carbonated beverages
- Coffee
- Energy drinks
- Soft drinks
- Tea with caffeine

Baked Goods
- Bagels
- Bread with yeast
- Cakes, cookies, desserts
- Muffins
- Rolls

Processed snack foods
- All crackers, chips, pretzels, bars, etc.

Sugar
- Agave
- Artificial sweeteners
- Honey
- Molasses
- Sugar, sucrose, etc.
- Syrup

Incorporate a variety of foods from the following categories in your meals throughout the day:

- Whole grains
- Leafy Greens
- Vegetables in a variety of colors
- Beans and legumes
- Healthy fats from olive oil, avocado, nuts, and seeds
- Fruit in moderation (2–3 cups a day)

Two Filters for the Daniel Fast

You may be ready to take the lists above and dive full force into grocery shopping and meal planning. If so, go for it! But for others, you may still have some questions. Like, "What about this particular item?" or, "Can I eat this kind of food?" Or maybe you're hearing conflicting advice about what's permissible to eat on a Daniel Fast.

You can answer the "what to eat" questions by choosing one of two primary filters. The purpose of the filters is to help you decide what grey-area foods (such as the infamous peanut butter) you will include when you're on a Daniel Fast.

The abstaining filter focuses primarily on what *not to eat*, and the limited filter focuses primarily on what you *will eat*. Ultimately, when using these filters, you will end up with a more comprehensive list of foods for your particular Daniel Fast than what's included in the charts in this chapter.

This section and the discussion of filters may seem nitpicky, but over the years, I've filtered lots of questions about specific food items. It's impossible to list every potential food item or ingredient, so it's better that you have a framework to make decisions. You can use the filters and FAQ section in the appendix to create your personal plan.

Which filter you choose may depend on your experience with fasting, your season of life, and the length of your fast. Remember it's important to consult your physician before making any drastic changes to your diet, and it's essential if you have any health conditions or take medication.

Abstaining filter

With the abstaining filter, you're primarily concerned with what to cut out of your diet—what not to eat. Start with the food lists above as a baseline and pay particular attention to the list of foods to abstain from.

Since your primary concern is to cut out the animal products, baked goods, beverages other than water, and processed snack foods while focusing on plant-based food, you may still eat items such as ready-made hummus, vegan protein powder, a veggie patty, or tofu stir-fry because, according to the way you're defining a Daniel Fast, these items are plant-based.

Here is a sample meal plan with the abstaining filter:

Breakfast

Baked Cherry Berry Oatmeal served with almond milk (see recipes)

Lunch

Veggie wrap—whole grain tortilla with hummus, veggies, and olives

Snack

Apple slices with almond butter

Dinner

Black bean veggie patty served on a green salad with tomato, bell peppers, and avocado

Limited filter

A limited filter is a more restrictive approach. Not only will you abstain from all the items previously mentioned, but you may cut out additional processed and prepackaged items. You might follow more stringent guidelines for eating only unprocessed vegetables, fruits, and whole grains direct from nature.

Some examples of decisions you might make with a more limited approach to the Daniel Fast would be: using only dried beans and not canned; making soups from scratch at home instead of purchasing canned or boxed soup from the store; or not including any kind of milk substitutes since they are processed and contain additives.

Here is a sample daily meal plan with a limited filter approach:

Breakfast

Steel-cut oats with walnuts and berries

Lunch

Green salad topped with fresh vegetables, beans, seeds, olive oil, and lemon dressing

Dinner

Sweet potato boats—stuffed with black beans, chopped bell pepper, onion, and corn

Garnish with avocado, cilantro, and lime

Ancient Daniel Fast

Here's a bonus option. Some people may be drawn to the idea of eating only what Daniel would have eaten. For this, you may need to put some more research into your food options, but they are pretty limited. You have to consider that most of our agricultural products and produce have been modified over time. Also, staples of our diet such as blueberries, sweet potatoes, and tropical fruits were all native to the Americas, so they would not have been eaten by Daniel.

There is a food list included earlier in this chapter of foods known to be eaten during biblical times, and here is a sample of what a day of eating might look like.

Breakfast

Apple, dried apricots, and almonds

Lunch

Green salad with cucumbers, tomatoes, chickpeas, and olives topped with lemon and olive oil

Grapes

Snack

Melon with mint

Dinner

Lentil Soup

Final Word

As we move on to meal planning and recipes, make sure to note the resources included in the appendix. One is a list of ingredients that are egg-based, milk-based, sweeteners, or contain yeast. The other is a list of frequently asked questions. This includes the food items most often asked about or under debate as to whether or not they can be included on a Daniel Fast.

If the abstaining versus limited filters seem confusing, don't overthink it. Just take the lists provided in this chapter and use them as your Daniel Fast guidelines when you go shopping or prepare meals. The most important things are to get started and remember that your spiritual steps are the more valuable part of this journey.

Fasting is a big step for some people, and it's a gigantic step for others. A Daniel Fast isn't about nitpicking every food item and ingredient and treating this as a diet plan that must be precisely followed to be effective. No, it is about your reason for fasting: to become closer to God.

Foods are not inherently bad or wrong as Paul told Timothy, "Everything created by God is good, and nothing is to be rejected if it is received with gratitude; for it is sanctified by means of the word of God and prayer." (1 Tim 4:4–5)

With that said, however, when you fast, you should be challenging your flesh and appetite, not trying to bend the rules. Fasting is not about taking the easiest path available but about growing through discipline. A Daniel Fast does require you to abstain from certain major food groups. With that in mind, enter your fast with a clear commitment of what you will and won't eat, and a conviction to stick to that plan when temptations come.

The sacrifice we make and the discipline we exercise are ultimately for our benefit. From a physical standpoint, the more pure and natural our diet is, the more we can cleanse and restore our bodies. As we limit indulgences, we grow stronger physically and spiritually.

As you read the following chapters and prepare your personal fasting plan, be honest with yourself. Are you purposefully choosing a food list that will allow you to cut corners? Or is it an appropriate level of challenge for you at this time? We all have to start somewhere, and you know what's best for you right now.

Decide in advance what you will eat, when you will eat, and why you will eat, and then stay committed.

Your Journey

Now is the time to get practical and determine exactly what you will be eating on your Daniel Fast. Go to danielfastjourney.com/bookresources to get printable food lists. Take a look at the resources in the appendices as well.

Chapter 7 Reflections

• How many servings of fruits and vegetables do you eat in a typical day? How will you start to incorporate more?

• Which of the items on the Daniel Fast food list do you normally eat, and which do you rarely or never eat?

• What filter (abstaining or limited) or parameters will you use for determining what foods to include on your Daniel Fast?

Chapter 8

Pack Your Bags: How to Prepare for a Daniel Fast

Then the Lord answered me and said: "Write the vision and make it plain on tablets, that he may run who reads it."—Hab 2:2

The best of all medicines is resting and fasting.—Benjamin Franklin

Have you ever committed to a new eating plan? If so, maybe you recognize this pattern. You launch with enthusiasm. You buy the book, tear a meal plan out of a magazine, or save recipes on Pinterest. The first several days start strong. You're in the kitchen trying new recipes, preparing lunches for the week, and feeling great.

But it takes no more than a few days before something pops up to derail you. Someone in the family gets sick. There's a surprise party at work, and you can't turn down a piece of cake. You come home exhausted, and you've run out of time and energy to make a new recipe.

Before you know it, a week or two has passed and everything is exactly back to normal. You're running through the drive-through and back to the same habits as before.

What went wrong? I've seen this scenario play out over the years not only with healthy eating plans but also with attempts to fast. I've realized the reason I fall off is not because of a lack of willpower; no, the main challenge is time. And it's the combination of time and energy. You can't underestimate the effort required to make changes in your lifestyle and eating habits. Also, it can be difficult to fit a one-size-fits-all plan into your unique personal situation.

When I get a new cookbook or eating plan, I look through the recipes and realize only a few sound appetizing for me and my family. Next, I take the time to assemble the ingredients from the various recipes into a shopping list. New recipes usually contain ingredients I don't have on hand. So my list is longer than usual, and I spend extra time tracking down random items in the store.

Then, every time I cook a new recipe, it takes extra effort. I have to carefully read all the steps to ensure I don't miss anything and stay focused on all the details. After several days of this, I'm ready for a break, and we end up ordering pizza.

We're all creatures of habit with habitual routines and behaviors. And we have also become accustomed to certain tastes, textures, and standards of eating, causing us to crave our comfort food—whatever is most familiar to us—whether that's noodle soup or mashed potatoes with gravy.

Our habits and natural cravings sometimes get the best of us. And on top of that, we combat decision fatigue, which is the deterioration of your ability to make good choices over time or when you're exhausted. The more you have on your plate, the more exhausted you will be. A complete eating overhaul takes a substantial amount of effort, but as you prepare for your Daniel Fast, you can follow the tips and tricks below to make the transition easier. Realizing that your greatest challenge may be time and energy, you can be strategic in meal planning, grocery shopping, and food preparation.

Repeat Meals

I don't know anyone who eats twenty-one different breakfasts, lunches, and dinners for three weeks. The average person repeats meals throughout the week and month, and this is wise because you don't have to buy an excessive variety of recipe ingredients or spend as much time preparing brandnew, meals each day.

Yet most diet books and meal plans feature a unique option at every meal. I think the good intention of this is to provide people with options and variety and to ensure they get their money's worth out of the book; however, it usually isn't practical to follow these meal plans exactly because of the effort, time, and decision fatigue previously mentioned.

Section four of this book provides a meal plan and recipes to give you a variety of ideas of what to eat. For the reasons listed above, it does contain unique recipes for each meal in the twenty-one-day plan, but there's also a rhythm that repeats each week. You can also take one week's meal plan and repeat it two or three times to avoid the number of new items you're preparing. Let's also discuss how to make a meal plan of your own.

Meal Planning

Having a clear plan for your Daniel Fast is essential. You should think through various scenarios you may encounter and how you will be prepared. For example, you need to know what you will order at a restaurant (check out the menu online in advance). If you're visiting a relative for the weekend, can you bring your own food along?

With those plans in place, you also need to plan for your daily eating at home. You will want a meal plan, and the best plan is the one you create for yourself.

Yes, meal planning requires an upfront time investment, but it saves you energy in the long run. When you create a plan and stock your kitchen, you won't have to wonder what's for dinner when five o'clock comes around. You can forget about that decision fatigue.

On the danielfastjourney.com/bookresources page, you'll find a blank meal plan template. To create your meal plan, walk through the following steps:

1. Inventory: Write down what you eat in a typical week for breakfast, lunch, snacks, and dinner. This can be an exact food record or based on your typical habits.

2. Assess: Are there plant-based foods and meals that can remain part of your Daniel Fast meal plan?

3. Substitute: Are there easy substitutions you could make so your meals fit the Daniel Fast?

4. Subtract: What meals or food items have to be taken out while you're on a Daniel Fast?

5. Add: What recipes and meals should you add? (Are there Daniel Fast friendly recipes you've used in the past? Can you test out a few dinner options before you begin?)

6. Also, as we talked about in a previous chapter, remember to plan out meals for your children or family members who won't be on the Daniel Fast with you.

Look for ways to make simple substitutions so you aren't working through completely new recipes in the kitchen for every meal. Maybe you eat oatmeal every morning or have a salad for lunch. You can adapt those meals to your Daniel Fast. You can eat an entree salad with beans instead of meat and substitute olive oil and lemon for your normal salad dressing. Or you can make stir-fry with vegetables and brown rice instead of fried rice and sesame chicken. You can take your tacos and turn them into a burrito bowl with rice, beans, and veggies on top.

I like to keep lunch simple by eating leftovers from the night before or sticking to soup or salad.

Trying new recipes can be fun, but isn't the main focus when you're fasting. You don't want to spend all your extra time in the kitchen. I make a general meal schedule and repeat it weekly so I'm not reinventing the wheel. Here is what that general plan could look like:

Sunday: Soup and salad (prepare large batches that can also be used for lunches)

Monday: Whole grain bowl with vegetables

Tuesday: Vegetable-based entree recipe

Wednesday: Entree salad with beans, nuts, and seeds

Thursday: Vegetable stew or chili

Friday: Vegetable-based entree recipe

Saturday: Stir-fry vegetables with rice

Grocery Shopping

The grocery store is not the ideal place to hang out when you're fasting. There's no need to torture yourself with the view of one hundred options of chips and the smell of fresh donuts. For that reason, you will want to reduce the number of trips you have to make to the store. A well-organized meal plan will help you do just that and also help you save time and money.

When shopping, stick to the store perimeter and avoid the bakery. You'll spend most of your time in the produce section selecting fruits and vegetables. On the grain aisle, look for 100 percent whole-grain items and brown rice. Make sure you read ingredient labels to ensure everything you purchase fits the Daniel Fast guidelines.

Frozen vegetables and fruits are also a great option. Most are pre-washed and cut, which is another timesaver. Frozen produce maintains its nutritional value because fruits and vegetables are frozen immediately following harvest. And you don't have to worry about them spoiling.

Fresh fruits and vegetables can ripen quickly, and you want to avoid wasting food. Check sell-by dates and reasonably estimate how much you will eat at a time before the food goes bad. Eating spinach at every meal is a noble-sounding idea, but is it really practical? Consider doing one major grocery trip for all dry goods needed for your fast, then shorter trips to pick up fresh produce for several days at a time.

Curbside grocery, pickup, and delivery are now common in most areas of the US. They are time efficient and can help you avoid in-store temptations, which are huge advantages! However, one challenge with these options is entrusting somebody else to pick out the best produce and double-check expiration dates. Taking a trip to the store will also give you the full scope of options available which can be difficult to gauge from an app or online platform. This can give you fresh ideas for new fruits and veggies to try. But it may take just one trip to the store, and then you're ready to save time with pick up or delivery options.

Batch Cooking

Batch work or time blocking is a great tool for increasing your productivity, and it can also apply to cooking. This is a productivity technique of grouping similar tasks together and completing them within the same timeframe. When it comes to cooking, this means picking a certain day and time to prepare several meals at once. It can also apply to food preparation.

For instance, the day you get home from the store, you can wash all your fruits and vegetables immediately before putting them in the refrigerator. The next day, you can chop and prep all the produce you'll need for recipes in the upcoming days. You can cook larger portions of grains like rice and quinoa to eat with multiple meals.

Some recipes can be cooked in bulk and frozen, and it helps to do this before you start your Daniel Fast. Soups tend to freeze well. You can make several batches of soup and freeze in individual portion sizes, which is a great option for lunch. The same is true for whole-grain bowls and stir-frys. Foods with high water content usually don't freeze well, so vegetables like salads or squash need to be prepared fresh.

You don't have to cook every night, although this may be customary. Cooking just a few days out of the week will maximize your time and energy, which is especially important when you're on a Daniel Fast. Some tips to take advantage of batch cooking include doing the following at the beginning of the week to set yourself up for multiple meals:

• Wash and cut fresh produce before you put it away.

- Prepare soup in large batches to be eaten for lunch or in addition to dinner entrees.

- Prepare a large batch of salad to be eaten multiple times for lunch or dinner. You can vary the toppings and add different nuts, seeds, fruits, olives, avocado, etc.

- Cook large batches of whole grains to use in recipes throughout the week. Options include: layer in bowls with toppings or stir-fry; stuff entrée-vegetables like bell peppers, avocados, and sweet potatoes; or eat for breakfast.

- Roast 1–2 pans of vegetables. Use roasted vegetables in salads, layer in bowls, or eat as a side dish.

- Prep recipe ingredients in advance: roast corn, trim bell peppers, cook sweet potatoes, chop herbs, etc.

- Ensure you have enough storage containers and consider storing individual portions.

The When, Where, and How of Eating

Beyond what you eat, it also matters when you eat, where you eat, and how you eat. Too often, we eat while scrolling through our phones, driving, or working. If you're multitasking, then you aren't aware of the quantity or quality of food, which leads to mindless overeating and constant snacking.

The Daniel Fast is defined by the types of food you eat, not necessarily how much, but this is the perfect time to become more mindful and intentional in your eating habits. Commit to only eat at planned mealtimes during your Daniel Fast. Eat sitting down, pray before each meal, then focus on the food in front of you and the other people around the table.

When you eat slowly and concentrate on what you're doing, you'll naturally consume less. A Daniel Fast should have defined mealtimes to avoid constant grazing throughout the day. That might be three meals and two snacks, but the point is to be intentional and plan what to eat and when.

Also, limit your meals to standard portions. Overeating does not reconcile with the spirit of fasting. So eat just enough to fuel yourself. This will also benefit your digestive system as it can function better when not constantly overloaded with food.

Every time you eat, check in with yourself and ask: Why am I eating right now? You should ask this same question when hunger and cravings hit. It's a key opportunity to get to the root of underlying issues that drive your eating habits.

- Are you eating because your stomach is empty, or are you bored?
- Are you hungry, or are you dehydrated because you aren't drinking enough water?
- Are you craving sugar and caffeine because you're exhausted from lack of sleep?

The goal of fasting is to shift from mindless grazing to mindful nourishment. To fill yourself spiritually rather than physically. Food is often our natural response to stress, celebration, or simple boredom.

Fasting forces us to check our motivations and uncover the real issues and encourages us to openly turn to God in prayer instead of scouring the pantry.

Blood sugar levels

When you're on a Daniel Fast, you should also consider how certain foods may affect your blood sugar. The glycemic index is a helpful tool. This concept was introduced in the 1980s to help diabetics control their blood sugar. Scientists have studied how foods with carbohydrates affect blood sugar based on how quickly they are digested. Blood sugar spikes can cause food cravings, mood swings, and energy crashes. For reference:

- High glycemic foods include cornflakes, white rice, and potatoes.
- Low glycemic foods include beans, apples, and steel-cut oats.

The goal is to choose foods with a low glycemic load as often as possible. You can find these food lists in books or on an Internet search; just be sure to look at reputable sources, like medical organizations or universities. If you eat foods that could spike your blood sugar, be sure to pair them with healthy fats or low glycemic items like beans or legumes.

The same principle applies to sugar in general. Although you shouldn't be eating any added sugars, you may be increasing your fruit intake on a Daniel Fast. Fruit contains fiber and fructose which has a different effect on the body than refined sugars, but it's still wise to consume moderate portions of fruit.

Fruits with the highest sugar content include cherries, mangoes, grapes, bananas, watermelon, and pineapple.

Fruits with the lowest sugar content include avocado, guava, strawberries, blueberries, grapefruit, lemons, and some apples.

Also, be mindful of portion sizes when eating dried fruit. Although dried fruit contains many fantastic nutrients, portion sizes are condensed compared to fresh fruit, so the sugar content adds up more quickly. Make sure you check ingredient labels of dried fruit, frozen fruit, and canned fruit to ensure there's no added sugar.

The average person doesn't need to be overly concerned about blood sugar effects as long as they're eating a balanced diet with a variety of different types of foods. Remember that beans and legumes are high in fiber and low in sugar. They will fill you up and should be a staple item on your Daniel Fast menu. Continue to eat a variety of foods, and follow the tips to transition into a Daniel Fast so your body has time to adjust.

Your Journey

As you get ready to start your Daniel Fast, consider the tips provided in this chapter and what will help you save time. Rather than reflection questions, it's time to plan it out.

1 - Complete your Daniel Fast meal plan.

2 - Create your shopping list and stock your pantry.

3 - Schedule your days for cooking and meal preparation.

Chapter 9

Continue the Journey: A Daniel Lifestyle

Then he continued, "Do not be afraid, Daniel. Since the first day that you set your mind to gain understanding and to humble yourself before your God, your words were heard, and I have come in response to them."—Dan 10:12

Fasting cleanses the soul, raises the mind, subjects one's flesh to the spirit, renders the heart contrite and humble, scatters the clouds of concupiscence, quenches the fire of lust, and kindles the true light of chastity —St. Augustine

One year in September, my husband and I decided to fast as we prayed for direction about his job situation. We had a two-year-old and a baby at the time. He was traveling frequently and in a high-pressure work environment. The entire situation was putting a load of anxiety and stress on both of us.

We prayed and fasted together for several days. While we didn't receive clear answers immediately, we ended the fast with a sense of peace and strengthened faith. Several weeks later, a former colleague of my husband reached out with a new job opportunity within the same company.

As we prayed and confirmed whether this was the right thing to do, we felt confident in our yes. We had fasted for clarity and an opportunity to open up, and there it was. Sometimes things fall too perfectly in place to be a coincidence.

Stories like this are encouraging. But I haven't always received a quick response or immediate confirmation every time I've fasted. Regardless, fasting is a way to mature in your faith and develop godly discipline. Discipline requires us to invest in the habits before we see the results.

As we carry on, the Daniel Fast can be a regular part of our lives. That could mean participating in an extended Daniel Fast at regular points throughout the year, or it could just mean you maintain certain eating principles you gleaned from the Daniel Fast in your daily diet or continue some of the spiritual disciplines you more diligently pursued while you were fasting every day.

You may find that when you reach the end of your time fasting, you're asking, "Now what's next?" This won't be the end of your journey. God may speak to you about your direction, the way you spend your time, or refresh you with a renewed sense of purpose.

The effects of a Daniel Fast aren't temporary; what you've experienced will impact you into the future. But you do need to commit to pressing forward and not going back on autopilot. If you fall back into the same spiritual routines and eating habits, you'll end up feeling the way you did before.

You may feel like Jamie, who left this comment on the blog a few years ago:

"Seriously, your meal plan recipes for the Daniel Fast actually made my husband and I go vegan after our Fast! Now we have a cheat day but we don't go crazy anymore and feel leaps and bounds better! Your meal plans helped us turn it into a lifestyle! Thanks!!!" (Jamie G)

Whether or not you're tempted to become vegan, consider how you'll continue your journey. You can fast at regular times throughout the year, and you can also apply these changes to your daily walk.

Walking the Walk

To quote the cliche, we don't just want to talk the talk, we want to be people who walk the walk. What does it look like to walk with God? This walk is more than a casual stroll, it's a purposeful manner of living.

The Greek word peripateō means, figuratively, the whole round of the activities of the individual life, whether of the unregenerate or the believer. [XXXII] It's not just the spiritual activities, but the way we talk to people, treat others, and go about our average day. The little things we do all the time matter as much, if not more, than the big things we do some of the time.

The great patriarchs and prophets of the Bible walked and conversed with God. In the gospels, Jesus called the disciples to follow Him. We are called to walk in a relationship with the Lord with the same conviction, stepping away from our former life and moving forward with Him. We have to decide who will be the primary influence on our thoughts and decisions: Will we listen to the world, ourselves, or Jesus?

You're probably familiar with the story of the Fall in Genesis chapter three. Satan tempts Eve to eat the forbidden fruit of the tree of the knowledge of good and evil, which she also gives to Adam. One detail of this story sticks out to me.

Verse eight says they hear the sound of the Lord walking in the garden in the cool of the day. Based on how easily they recognize and respond, it's clear that walking with God was a regular occurrence, not a rare incident. Can you imagine being so close to the Lord's presence that you walk with Him in a tangible way every day?

He's a God of relationship. He wants to have the closeness with each of us that He had with the patriarchs of the Old Testament including Noah, Abraham, and Moses. Or Enoch. Genesis 5:24 says, "Enoch walked with God; and he was not, for God took him." He lived 365 years, so this was not a couple of random evening strolls but a full lifetime dedicated to living with God. As God spoke directly to these men, He gave them directives that impacted their families and legacies for generations.

When you reach the end of your life, will the people closest to you be able to say "she walked with God"?

If that's not the case, consider what small elements of your daily walk you can dedicate to the Lord. As fasting teaches us, we can't rely solely on our ability to do good or the strength of our willpower. As we grow and mature, we don't become less dependent on God, we actually become more dependent on Him. In your quiet moments with God, you receive the truth you need to change, the fuel to sustain you, and the courage to continue even when facing obstacles.

Regular periods of fasting can strengthen our spirit, help us draw closer to the Lord, and improve our physical health. But the ultimate goal is not personal benefit. As we refresh our spirits and renew our minds, our perspective and priorities shift. The focus may start with our personal well-being, but eventually extends beyond ourselves.

We can step out of introspection and consider how we can serve others. As we draw closer to the Lord, our spiritual tank fills up and we find ourselves healthier and stronger. Now we're ready and eager to ask that "what's next" question.

Finding your purpose can sound like a larger than life and overwhelming task. Purpose is a big word, with lots of weight attached. But purpose doesn't have to be a grand lifetime project. It doesn't necessarily have to be specific to our jobs and careers. Purpose can be found in all the small moments as we walk with God, loving Him, and loving others.

Our purpose is found in following the great commandment we talked about earlier:

"And you shall love the Lord your God with all your heart, and with all your soul, and with all your mind, and with all your strength. The second is this, 'you shall love your neighbor as yourself.' There is no other commandment greater than these."

(Mark 12:30–31)

Journey Checkpoints

As you continue, remember the importance of fasting as a checkpoint on your journey. These times of fasting can be a regular pause and opportunity for assessment and reflection. When you fast, remember to check your compass, your pace, and your supplies.

Your compass reveals what direction you're headed. We are prone to drift and wander from our best intentions. Although we may get sidetracked by distractions and difficulties, when we fast, we recalibrate and return our attention to our main focus.

Just as we can lose our sense of direction, we can also lose our steady pace. We may find ourselves stalled out, sitting by the side of the road and lacking motivation. Or we may be going too fast, finding ourselves yet again frantically scurrying in the hamster wheel.

Everyone has a different pace, so be careful not to compare yourself to the family next door or the coworker in the next cubicle. Some people can sustain a moderate jog, while others need to stick to a brisk walk.

Your pace will also change through different seasons. You can't formulate a one-time plan or schedule to last ten years. As your kids mature, you grow older, and the environment around you shifts, your plan may need to change. But through it all, the habit of fasting will help you remember to seek God for the season you're in.

When examining your pace, consider whether you have margin in your life. Have you created room to breathe? This is also where you can check your level of supplies and whether you're operating from a full tank or running on fumes.

In the Old Testament, the priests were charged with keeping the fire burning on the altar at all times and not letting it go out (Lev 6:12). If our fire is getting weak, it's time to clear away anything that might be smothering it and find some good, clean fuel to reignite it.

We need fresh bread and living water every day. After leaving slavery in Egypt, God gave the Israelites manna every morning. They couldn't stockpile an extra supply; they had to gather just what they needed and trust God's daily provision. "They gathered it morning by morning, every man as much as he should eat." (Exod 16:21)

Jesus calls Himself the living bread in the New Testament. He also tells His disciples to pray: give us this day our daily bread. Becoming spiritually depleted and dehydrated is dangerous. We can't rely on others to nourish us or expect a sporadic feeding to sustain us.

Our spirit, soul, and body need to be replenished regularly. Learn to recognize when your internal resources are running low. Then take the time to rest and restore yourself.

Well Life

Wellness is about more than what you eat, it's also about what you think, the care of your soul, and how you live. It's not enough to get the right meal plan or to read about the need to exercise for thirty minutes a day. The challenge is to actually put healthy habits into practice consistently.

The missing link, as we've talked about, is approaching your health holistically. You are a spirit, soul, and body. These parts are intimately intertwined, interconnected, and influencing each other. Thus, you should pursue health on all fronts. The cliche a *rising tide lifts all boats* applies to wellness!

What happens when you prioritize your health? You could decide spiritually to focus on more Bible study or physically to improve your strength with a new exercise program. You might commit to practicing gratitude and having a healthier thought life. Whatever your goal, a baseline of healthy habits will help you succeed long-term.

I'm convinced that people could drastically and immediately shift their perspective and improve their overall well-being if they would focus on five simple, daily physical health practices:

1. Get 7–9 hours of quality sleep each night.

2. Drink enough water (and drink primarily water).

3. Get thirty minutes a day of moderate physical activity.

4. Get outside and expose yourself to morning and evening sunlight. Sunshine is a source of vitamin D and helps to regulate hormones, Circadian rhythms, and sleep.

5. Have a stress-relief practice. It could be deep breathing for five minutes a day, journaling, gratitude, or someone you talk to. But find a healthy way to manage and respond to stress.

Living well can be a challenge because we are surrounded by temptations and unhealthy choices. As we go throughout our day, we can dismiss small choices and decisions as being irrelevant. But over time, the accumulation of these choices forms who we are. At every opportunity, make a good choice—whether that's what you eat for dinner or a random act of kindness to a stranger.

Fasting teaches us to endure temporary discomfort and keep our eye on the prize. Temporary satisfaction cannot measure up to the greater rewards we have available to us as believers. Fasting is about seeing with God's eyes and drawing close to His heart.

PART FIVE
RECIPE GUIDE

Meal Plan and Recipe Introduction

When I fast, my goal is simplicity, not creating decadent and delicious meals. When you cook in bulk and repeat simple meals, you'll spend less time in the kitchen and have more time to invest elsewhere.

This section contains a twenty-one-day meal plan with recipe options. If you've skipped straight to this section, be sure to visit the tips in chapter eight for how to create your meal plan and save time cooking. As mentioned there, it's not necessary to eat a different meal for every breakfast, lunch, and dinner over the course of twenty-one days (and perhaps not practical). At danielfastjourney. com/bookresources, you can download a template for planning your meals.

With that said, this section does contain a twenty-one-day meal plan with unique options to showcase a variety of recipes. Some of these are variations on a theme, such as whole grain vegetable bowls. You can find additional recipes in vegan cookbooks, blogs, and on the danielfastjourney.com website. As you find these recipes, be sure to check the ingredients to include only Daniel Fast foods. The substitutions below can also help you to adapt recipes to a Daniel Fast.

Remember to keep it simple and eat to live, not live to eat.

Recipe Substitutions

Your favorite meatless dishes may still contain animal-based ingredients like butter or eggs. If you would like to adapt one of your favorite recipes or something you've found outside this book, below is a list of substitutions.

The substitution may vary depending on whether the dish is savory or sweet. For example, sometimes avocado or olive oil is a better flavor for a savory dish than coconut oil. Mashed bananas can be a good egg substitute for a breakfast dish, but chia seeds may taste better in a savory-based dish.

Plant-based alternatives

For Butter
- Avocado Oil
- Avocado
- Coconut Oil

For Eggs
Egg substitute for binding and thickening:

• Chia seed: Combine 1 tbs. chia seeds and 3 tbs. water, stir, and allow to sit for 10–15 minutes until consistency thickens

• Flaxseed: Combine 1 tbs. flax seeds and 3 tbs. water, stir, and allow to sit for 10–15 minutes

• 2 tbs. mashed potatoes

Egg substitute for moisture:

• ¼ cup mashed banana

• ¼ cup pumpkin purée

• ¼ cup unsweetened applesauce

• 2 tbs. tomato paste (savory dishes)

For Milk

Can be used in a 1:1 ratio

• Almond milk

• Coconut milk

• Oat milk

• Rice milk

For Yogurt

• Coconut Cream—refrigerate for several hours, then skim the cream off the top

• Cashew Yogurt—soak ½ cup of raw cashews in ¾ cup water for 30 minutes, then blend to a smooth paste

• Silken tofu blended (if consuming tofu)

21 DAY MEAL PLAN

Add a cup of soup, salad, side of veggies, fruit or whole grains on the side of any of the following for a more filling and complete meal. See the Daniel Fast Journey book for recipe

WEEK 1 MEAL PLAN

	BREAKFAST	LUNCH	DINNER
DAY 1	Steel Cut Oats with berries and nuts	Green Salad topped with beans	Lentil Soup
DAY 2	Savory Breakfast Potatoes	Lentil Soup (leftover)	Asian Salad
DAY 3	Fruit and Veggie Smoothie	Black Bean and Mango Lettuce Wrap	Cashew Chickpea Curry
DAY 4	Tropical Fruit and Nut Bowl	Whole Grain Bowl	Old Fashioned Vegetable Soup
DAY 5	Brown Rice Porridge	Vegetable Soup (leftover)	Southwest Whole Grain Bowl
DAY 6	Baked Apple Cinnamon Steel Cut Oats	Bulgur Salad with Carrots and Cilantro	Mediterranean Stuffed Bell Peppers
DAY 7	Fruit and Veggie Smoothie	Pearl Couscous with Roasted Tomatoes	Stir Fry (any combo) over Brown Rice

21 DAY MEAL PLAN

WEEK 2 MEAL PLAN

	BREAKFAST	LUNCH	DINNER
DAY 1	Steel Cut Oats with berries and nuts	Green Salad topped with beans	White Bean and Spinach Soup
DAY 2	Sweet Potato and Apple Hash	White Bean and Spinach Soup (leftover)	Mediterranean Salad
DAY 3	Fruit and Veggie Smoothie	Stir Fry Vegetables over rice	Portabella Mushroom Caps
DAY 4	Berry Fruit and Nut Bowl	Quinoa Stuffed Avocados	Corn Chowder with Sweet Potato
DAY 5	Overnight Berry Quinoa Porridge	Corn Chowder (leftover)	Mediterranean Farro Whole Grain Bowl
DAY 6	Baked Pumpkin Oatmeal	Hummus Lettuce Wrap	Easy Roasted Vegetables over Quinoa
DAY 7	Fruit and Veggie Smoothie	Stir Fry (any combo) over Brown Rice	Vegetable Paella

21 DAY MEAL PLAN

WEEK 3 MEAL PLAN

	BREAKFAST	LUNCH	DINNER
DAY 1	Steel Cut Oats with berries and nuts	Green Salad topped with beans	Tomato Rice Soup
DAY 2	Veggie Breakfast Bowl	Tomato Rice Soup (leftover)	Southwest Salad
DAY 3	Fruit and Veggie Smoothie	Cashew Lettuce Wraps	Southwest Corn and Black Bean Sweet Potatoes
DAY 4	Harvest Fruit and Nut Bowl	Whole Grain Bowl (any combo)	3 Bean Vegan Chili
DAY 5	Breakfast Farro with Spinach	3 Bean Chili (leftover)	Roasted Veggie & Bulgur Whole Grain Bowl
DAY 6	Baked Apple Cherry Berry Oatmeal	Chickpea and Quinoa Salad	Spaghetti Squash with Tomato Sauce
DAY 7	Fruit and Veggie Smoothie	Roasted Eggplant Stacks	Stir Fry (any combo) over brown rice

Recipe Contents

Page Number and Recipe

LUNCH AND DINNER

Soups

Salads

Salad Dressings

Whole Grains

Breakfast

Oatmeal

Oatmeal is a common breakfast item and easy to prepare. Less processed oats have greater nutritional value, so try to stick with steel-cut oats on a Daniel Fast. They have become so common that you can even purchase steel-cut oats at some fast-food restaurants and popular coffee chains. The progression from most processed to least processed oatmeal is:

1. Instant Oatmeal
2. Quick Oats
3. Rolled Oats
4. Steel-Cut Oats or Irish Oatmeal

Below are several cooking methods and topping options. Because oatmeal is so easy to make and familiar, it's usually a staple breakfast item.

Oatmeal Prep Methods

Steel-Cut Oats: Stovetop Prep

Serves 2

- ½ cup steel-cut oats
- 1 ½ cups water

1. Bring 1 ½ cups of water to a boil in a large saucepan.
2. Stir in ½ cup of steel-cut oats.
3. Reduce heat to low and simmer for 10–15 minutes, stirring regularly until liquid is absorbed and oatmeal thickens.
4. Remove from heat and allow to stand for 5 minutes.

Steel-Cut Oats: Slow Cooker Prep

Serves 4

- Coconut oil
- 3 ½ cups water
- 1 cup steel-cut oats

1. Lightly spray or wipe slow cooker with coconut oil.
2. Combine water and steel-cut oats in slow cooker.
3. Cover and cook on low or warm setting for 6–7 hours.

4. Remove lid and stir to combine ingredients that may have separated while cooking.

5. Portion into bowls and add any desired toppings.

Notes: Overnight slow cooker oatmeal will not work with quick-cooking or rolled oats as they will become too mushy.

Steel-Cut Oats: Instant Pot Prep

Serves 4

- Coconut oil
- 4 cups water or non-dairy milk substitute
- 1 cup steel-cut oats

1. Lightly spray or coat Instant Pot liner with coconut oil.

2. Combine water or non-dairy milk and steel-cut oats in Instant Pot and stir.

3. Close lid securely and set pressure release valve to Sealing.

4. Select high-pressure cook setting, and set timer for 12 minutes.

5. When cooking is complete, allow natural pressure release for 20 minutes, then move pressure release valve to Venting to release all remaining steam.

6. Remove lid, stir to combine, portion into bowls, and add any desired toppings.

Notes for Slow Cooker and Instant Pot Prep:

• Toppings can be added at step 2 or after cooking.

• Gluten-free oats can be used in these recipes.

• If there is extra water after cooking, stir and allow to stand for several minutes to reabsorb water before serving.

• If oatmeal is too thick, hot water or additional milk substitute can be added.

• Cooked oats can be stored for one week or frozen for up to two months.

Oatmeal Topping Variations

Apple Walnut

• 1 medium apple, cored and diced

• ½ cup unsweetened natural applesauce

• ½ tsp ground ginger

• 1 tsp ground cinnamon

• 2 tbs. walnuts

Banana Nut

• 1 small–medium banana, sliced

• 1 tsp ground cinnamon

• 2 tbs. walnuts

Berry Blend

- ¼ cup blueberries
- ¼ cup sliced strawberries
- ¼ cup unsalted almonds
- 1 tbs. golden raisins

Promised Land Blend

- 1 tbs. dates, chopped
- 1 tbs. figs, chopped
- 1 tbs. raisins
- 1 tbs. ground flax seeds
- ¼ cup unsalted almonds

Baked Oatmeal

Baked Apple Cinnamon Oatmeal

Serves 4

- 1 cup steel-cut oats
- 3 cups almond, coconut, or oat milk
- 2 medium, ripe bananas
- 1 apple, chopped
- ½ cup raisins (optional)

- 1 tsp vanilla extract
- 1 tsp ground cinnamon
- ½ tsp sea salt
- Coconut oil or spray

1. Preheat oven to 350 degrees.

2. Coat 8x8 baking dish with coconut oil.

3. Mash bananas with a fork.

4. Mix all ingredients and spread in baking dish.

5. Bake covered for 45 minutes, then uncovered for 15 minutes.

6. Cut into squares and serve with fresh fruit and chopped nuts if desired.

Notes:

- To substitute rolled oats in this recipe, use 2 cups oats and reduce bake time to 35–40 minutes

- To make oatmeal cups, prepare a muffin tin, preheat oven to 375 degrees, and cook 15–20 minutes

Baked Pumpkin Oatmeal

Serves 4

- 1 cup steel-cut oats
- 1 flax egg (1 tbs. flax seed + 3 tbs. water)
- 2 cups oat milk or other milk substitute

- ¾ cup pumpkin purée
- 2 tbs. coconut oil
- 1 tsp vanilla extract
- ½ tsp ground cinnamon
- ¼ tsp ground ginger
- ¼ tsp ground nutmeg
- 1 tsp baking powder
- ¾ tsp salt
- ½ cup pecans, chopped

1. Preheat oven to 350 degrees.
2. Coat 8x8 baking dish with coconut oil.
3. Combine flax seeds and water, and let stand for 10–15 minutes.
4. Mix flax egg, oat milk, and pumpkin purée, then add coconut oil and vanilla extract.
5. In a separate bowl, stir together dry ingredients then add to pumpkin mixture.
6. Stir until combined then pour into baking dish.
7. Bake 45–50 minutes.
8. Cool and cut into squares, serve with desired toppings.

Baked Cherry Berry Oatmeal

Serves 4–6

- 1 cup steel-cut oats
- 3 cups almond, coconut, or oat milk
- 1 tbs. chia seeds + 3 tbs. water
- 1 cup frozen cherries, pitted
- ½ cup frozen or fresh blueberries
- ½ tsp vanilla
- ½ tsp cinnamon
- ¼ tsp sea salt
- Coconut oil or spray

1. Preheat oven to 350 degrees.
2. Coat 8x8 baking dish with coconut oil.
3. Combine chia seeds and water and let stand for 10–15 minutes.
4. Mix all ingredients and place in baking dish.
5. Bake for 50–60 minutes.
6. Allow to cool 15–30 minutes.

Serve immediately for a softer texture or allow to set overnight. Serve warm or cold.

Breakfast Whole Grains

Brown Rice Porridge

Serves 2

- 1 ½ cups brown rice, cooked
- ¾ cup unsweetened almond, rice, or coconut milk
- 2 tbs. ground flaxseed
- 2 tbs. raisins
- ½ tsp cinnamon
- 1 pinch sea salt

1. Combine all ingredients in a medium-size saucepan.

2. Bring to a gentle boil on medium heat, stirring frequently.

3. Lower to a simmer and cook for 2–3 minutes or until desired consistency is reached, continuing to stir frequently to avoid sticking.

4. Remove from heat and portion into bowls, adding desired toppings.

Topping ideas:

-Almonds, walnuts, or pecans

-Dried fruit

-Coconut (flakes or shredded)

-Berries or fresh fruit

-Chia seeds

Overnight Berry Quinoa Porridge

Serves 2

- ½ cup dry quinoa, rinsed
- 1 cup almond milk
- 1 cup mixed berries, fresh or frozen
- 1 tbs. almond butter
- ½ banana

1. Combine all ingredients (berries and banana optional) in a slow cooker.
2. Cook on low 6–7 hours.
3. Serve warm, topped with almonds and fresh fruit.

Notes: If you dislike the texture or flavor of cooked fruit, you can leave the berries and banana to be added at the end.

Breakfast Farro with Spinach and Mushrooms

Serves 2

- 1 cup cooked farro
- 1 cup mushrooms, sliced
- 2 cups fresh baby spinach
- 1 small clove garlic, minced
- 1 cup cherry or grape tomatoes, halved

- 1 tbs. fresh parsley
- ½ tsp sea salt
- 1 tbs. olive oil
- Lemon wedges (optional)

1. Heat olive oil in a skillet over medium-high heat.

2. Add mushrooms and cook for 4–5 minutes.

3. Add garlic and cook for approximately 2 minutes, stirring to prevent sticking or burning.

4. Add spinach and continue cooking until wilted but not overdone.

5. Portion farro into bowls and top with spinach-mushroom mixture. Top with halved cherry tomatoes and sprinkle sea salt and chopped, fresh parsley on the top. Finish with a squeeze of fresh lemon.

Notes:

- See "Whole Grain" section for instructions on cooking farro.
- Farro can be made in advance and stored in the refrigerator for a couple of days.

Breakfast Potatoes and Veggies

Savory Breakfast Potatoes

Serves 2

- 1 tbs. olive oil
- 2 cups red or gold potatoes, diced
- ½ red or yellow bell pepper, diced
- ¼ yellow onion, diced
- ½ tsp garlic powder
- ½ tsp sea salt
- 2 tbs. fresh dill or rosemary
- 2 tbs. fresh parsley

1. Preheat oven to 400 degrees.

2. Line a sheet pan with foil or a silicone baking mat.

3. Combine potatoes, bell pepper, and onions and toss with olive oil.

4. Sprinkle garlic powder, sea salt, and dill or rosemary to coat evenly.

5. Bake for 40–50 minutes, until potatoes are tender when pierced with a fork.

6. Cool slightly and garnish with fresh parsley.

Sweet Potato and Apple Breakfast Hash

Serves 2

- 1 large sweet potato, diced in even chunks
- 2 small apples, chopped (Granny Smith or other)
- ¼ cup yellow onion, chopped
- ½ tsp garlic powder
- ½ tsp dried sage (optional)
- ½ tsp sea salt
- 2–3 tsp coconut oil

1. Preheat oven to 400 degrees.

2. Toss sweet potato chunks with 1 tsp coconut oil and salt.

3. Spread evenly on a baking sheet and roast 10–12 minutes until partially cooked but still firm.

4. Heat remaining 1–2 tsp coconut oil in a skillet, and sauté onion for 3–4 minutes.

5. Add chopped apples and sauté for an additional 3–4 minutes.

6. Add sweet potatoes, garlic powder, and sage (optional) and continue to cook, stirring occasionally, until sweet potatoes are fully done.

Notes:

- Apples can be peeled or the skin left on. Wait until cooking time to chop apples so they don't brown.

• Other vegetables like Brussels sprouts and carrots can be added in step 2 if desired.

• You can use leftover roasted sweet potatoes. Skip the first three steps and add cooked sweet potatoes at step six.

Veggie Breakfast Bowl

Serves 2

- 1 tbs. olive oil
- ½ cup cooked quinoa
- ¼ cup yellow onion, diced
- ½ cup red and yellow bell peppers, thinly sliced
- ½ cup broccoli, chopped into small pieces
- ½ cup sliced mushrooms
- 1 cup fresh spinach
- ½ tsp garlic powder
- ¼ tsp sea salt
- 1 avocado
- Green onions for garnish

1. Heat olive oil in a skillet over medium heat.
2. Cook onion for 2–3 minutes, then add in pepper, broccoli, and mushrooms, cooking each layer for a few additional minutes.
3. Add garlic powder and sea salt and stir, cooking until all vegetables are tender.

4. Add in cooked quinoa and stir until heated through.

5. Add spinach and cook until just wilted.

6. Remove from heat, portion into bowls, and top with sliced avocado and sliced green onions.

Fruit & Nut Bowls

Berry Fruit and Nut Bowl

Serves 1

- ½ cup mixed berries (blueberries, raspberries, blackberries, strawberries)
- ½ banana, sliced
- ¼ cup raw, unsalted almonds and walnuts
- 1 tbs. golden raisins
- 1 tbs. chia seeds
- 1 tbs. ground flax seeds

Layer all ingredients in a bowl and enjoy!

Tropical Fruit and Nut Bowl

Serves 1

- ¼ cup chopped pineapple (fresh or frozen)
- ¼ cup chopped mango
- 1 kiwi, sliced
- ¼ cup raw, unsalted cashews
- 1 tbs. coconut flakes
- 1 tbs. chia seeds

Layer all ingredients in a bowl and enjoy!

Harvest Fruit and Nut Bowl

Serves 1

- ½ cup pears, chopped
- ¼ cup frozen cherries, thawed
- ¼ cup walnuts
- 1 tbs. raisins
- 1 tbs. ground flaxseed
- Dash of ground cinnamon

Layer all ingredients in a bowl and enjoy!

*These are great options for breakfast, lunch, or snacks

Smoothies

Smoothies are a great option for breakfast, lunch, or snacks. You can create any combo you like, but here are some suggestions. A high-powered blender is advantageous for ensuring your smoothies come out "smooth." You can also add water or strain out seeds.

Triple Berry Green Smoothie

Serves 1

- ½ cup water
- ½ cup strawberries, fresh or frozen
- ½ cup blueberries, fresh or frozen
- ½ cup raspberries, fresh or frozen
- 1 cup fresh spinach
- 1 tbs. chia seeds
- 2-3 ice cubes

Blend all ingredients thoroughly and enjoy.

Gorgeous Greens Smoothie

Serves 1

- ½ cup water
- ½ cup strawberries, fresh or frozen
- ½ cucumber, peeled and chopped

- 1 cup fresh kale or spinach
- 2-3 ice cubes

Blend all ingredients thoroughly and enjoy.

Rise and Shine Smoothie

Serves 1

- ½ cup water
- ½ orange, peeled and chopped
- ½ cup raspberries, fresh or frozen
- ½ cup carrots, peeled and chopped
- 2-3 ice cubes

Blend all ingredients thoroughly and enjoy.

Great Grape Smoothie

Serves 1

- ½ cup grapes, red or green
- ½ orange, peeled and chopped
- ½ cup pineapple, chopped
- 1 cup fresh spinach
- 2-3 ice cubes

Blend all ingredients thoroughly and enjoy.

Veggie-ful Smoothie

Serves 1

- ½ cup grapes, red or green
- ½ orange, peeled and chopped
- ½ apple, chopped
- ½ medium carrot, peeled and chopped
- ½ cup fresh broccoli, chopped
- 1 cup fresh kale or spinach
- 2–3 ice cubes

Blend all ingredients thoroughly and enjoy.

Cucumber Melon Smoothie

Serves 1

- ½ cup water
- ½ cup grapes, red or green
- 1 cup melon (cantaloupe, honeydew, or combo)
- ½ cucumber, peeled and chopped
- ½ lime, peeled
- 2–3 ice cubes

Blend all ingredients thoroughly and enjoy.

Lunch and dinner

Quinoa Stuffed Avocados

Serves 2–4

- 2 cups quinoa, cooked
- ¼ cup red onion, diced small
- ½ cup cucumber, diced
- ½ cup tomatoes, diced
- 2 tbs. fresh cilantro, chopped
- 2 tbs. olive oil
- ½ tsp salt
- 4 avocados, halved and pitted

1. Prepare quinoa according to package directions. Fluff with a fork and transfer to a large bowl. Mix the quinoa with the red onion, cucumber, tomatoes, cilantro, olive oil, and salt.

2. Cut each avocado in half, remove the pit, and gently scoop out half of the avocado flesh, chop and set aside.

3. Scoop the quinoa salad into the center of each avocado and top with fresh chopped avocado. Serve immediately.

Roasted Eggplant Stacks

Serves 2-3

- 1 medium eggplant, sliced ½ inch thick
- 8 oz. marinara sauce
- 1 cup fresh spinach
- ½ tsp dried parsley
- ½ tsp dried basil
- 1–2 tbs. olive oil
- Salt and pepper to taste

Cashew Ricotta

- ¾ cups raw cashews
- ½ cup water
- ½ lemon, juiced
- 1 garlic clove, minced
- ¼ tsp salt
- ¼ tsp onion powder

1. Soak cashews in water for 2 hours until soft. Drain and add additional ricotta ingredients: water, lemon juice, garlic, salt, and onion powder. Blend until creamy.

2. Preheat oven to 400 degrees. Line baking sheet with foil or baking mat and drizzle with olive oil. Place eggplant slices on sheet, season with salt and pepper, and roast for approximately 20 minutes. Flip over and cook an additional 15 minutes or until done. Cool slightly.

3. Heat approximately 1 tbs. olive oil in a skillet over medium heat. Sauté spinach, dried parsley, and dried basil.

4. Stack eggplant slices, marinara sauce, and spinach mixture two times, then finish with a dollop of cashew ricotta on the top.

Black Bean and Mango Lettuce Wrap

Serves 2

- Large romaine or butter lettuce leaves
- ½ cup black beans, drained
- ¼ cup corn
- ¼ cup red bell pepper, chopped
- ¼ cup mango, chopped
- 2 tbs. red onion, finely chopped
- Olive oil
- Salt and pepper to taste
- ¼ cup grape or cherry tomatoes, chopped

- ½ avocado, chopped
- 2 tbs. fresh cilantro

1. Thoroughly wash lettuce and pat dry.

2. Combine black beans, corn, red bell pepper, mango, and red onion in a bowl. Drizzle with olive oil and salt and pepper to taste.

3. Spoon black bean mixture onto lettuce leaves and top with tomatoes, avocados, and cilantro.

Notes: The number of lettuce leaves you use in these lettuce wrap recipes will depend on the size of the leaves and how much filling you like in each.

Hummus Lettuce Wrap

Serves 2

- Large romaine or other large lettuce leaves
- 2 tbs. hummus (any flavor)
- ½ cup cucumber, chopped
- ½ cup cherry or grape tomatoes, halved
- 2 tbs. kalamata olives, sliced
- 2 tbs. red onion, finely sliced (optional)

1.Thoroughly wash lettuce and pat dry.

2.Evenly distribute ingredients in the lettuce leaves: hummus, cucumber, tomatoes, olives, and onion.

Cashew Lettuce Wrap

Serves 2

- Large romaine or other large lettuce leaves
- 1 cup brown rice or quinoa, cooked
- ½ cup shredded cabbage (mixed green and purple)
- ¼ cup shredded carrots
- ½ cup peas
- ½ cup mandarin oranges
- ¼ cup cashews
- 2 tbs. green onions, sliced
- ½ fresh lime (optional)

1. Thoroughly wash lettuce and pat dry.

2. Evenly distribute ingredients in the lettuce leaves: rice, cabbage, carrots, peas, mandarin oranges. Top with cashews, green onion, and a squeeze of fresh lime.

Soups

Lentil Soup

Serves approx. 6

- 1–2 tbs. olive oil
- 1 medium onion, finely chopped
- 2 medium carrots, peeled and chopped
- 3 garlic cloves, minced
- ½ tsp dried thyme
- 14.5 oz. can diced tomatoes
- 1 bay leaf
- 1 cup lentils, rinsed and picked over
- 5 cups vegetable broth
- 1 ½ cups water
- ¼ cup fresh parsley, minced
- ½ fresh lemon
- Salt and pepper

1. Heat olive oil in a large pot or Dutch oven over medium heat, add onion and carrots and cook for about 3 minutes. Add garlic and thyme and cook for 30 seconds, stirring constantly. Stir in tomatoes and bay leaf, and cook for another 30 seconds.

2. Stir in lentils, reduce heat to low, and cook until vegetables are soft about 8–10 minutes.

3. Add broth and water, increase heat and bring to a boil. Cover pot, reduce heat to low, and simmer about 30 minutes or until lentils are tender.

4. Remove bay leaf and discard. Process 3 cups of soup in a blender (or use an immersion blender) then return to pot and reheat over low heat. Add additional broth or water if needed. Season with salt and pepper, stir in parsley and lemon juice and serve.

White Bean and Spinach Soup

Serves 6–8

- 1 ½ cups dried Cannellini (white) beans
- 2 tbs. olive oil
- 1 cup onion, chopped
- 4 celery ribs, sliced
- ¾ tsp dried oregano
- 32 oz. vegetable broth
- 6 oz. spinach
- 3 tbs. fresh lemon juice
- 2 tbs. parsley, chopped
- Salt & pepper

1. Sort and pick through beans. Dissolve 3 tbs. salt in 4 quarts of cold water in a large pot or container and soak beans in water at room temperature for 8–24 hours. Drain and rinse.

2. Heat oil in large pot and sauté onion with ½ tsp of salt and ½ tsp of pepper for approximately 5 minutes. Stir in oregano, celery, broth, and soaked beans and bring to a boil.

3. Reduce heat to low and simmer 50–60 minutes or until beans are tender to taste.

4. Remove 2 cups of soup and process in a blender or food processor until smooth. Return to pot and heat soup over medium-low heat. Add more broth or liquid if desired.

5. Add spinach and stir until wilted. Stir in lemon juice, parsley, and salt and pepper to taste.

Tomato Rice Soup

Serves approx 6
- 2 tbs. olive oil
- 2 medium carrots, chopped
- 1 medium stalk celery, chopped
- 2–3 garlic cloves, chopped
- 1 cup yellow onion, chopped
- 1 tbs. tomato paste
- 32 oz. vegetable stock
- 1 cup brown rice, cooked
- 1 28 oz. can diced tomatoes
- 2 tbs. fresh parsley, chopped
- 2 tbs. fresh basil, chopped

• Salt and pepper

1. Heat olive oil in a large pot. Add carrots, celery, and onions and cook for about 5 minutes, until vegetables are tender. Add garlic and cook an additional 30 seconds, stirring. Add tomato paste and stir 30–60 seconds more.

2. Add vegetable stock and diced tomatoes. Bring to a boil over medium-high heat, stirring occasionally and breaking up tomatoes.

3. Reduce heat to low, add rice and simmer gently for about 20 minutes. Add parsley, basil, and salt and pepper to taste.

Old Fashioned Vegetable Soup

Serves 6–8

• 2 tbs. olive oil
• 1 yellow onion, chopped
• 4 medium carrots, chopped
• 3 ribs celery, chopped
• 4 cloves garlic, finely chopped
• ½ tsp dried thyme
• ½ tsp dried oregano
• 1 tsp salt
• 4–6 cups vegetable broth
• 28 oz. can diced tomatoes
• 3 medium potatoes, peeled and cut into even cubes

- 2 bay leaves
- ¼ cup fresh parsley, chopped (additional for garnish)
- 1 cup frozen green beans
- 1 cup frozen corn
- 1 cup frozen peas

1. Heat olive oil in a large pot and cook onion, carrots, and celery for about 5 minutes. Add garlic, thyme, oregano, and salt and cook 30–60 seconds more.

2. Add broth, tomatoes, potatoes, bay leaves, and parsley then heat to boiling.

3. Reduce heat to low, cover, and simmer about 20 minutes, testing potatoes for doneness.

4. Increase heat to medium-high, add green beans, corn, and peas then cook an additional 5–10 minutes. Test vegetables for doneness.

5. Season with salt and pepper to taste and serve topped with fresh parsley.

Notes: You can substitute a frozen vegetable mix of carrots, corn, and peas rather than add individually.

Corn Chowder with Sweet Potato

Serves 6–8

- 1 tbs. olive oil
- 1 yellow onion, chopped
- 1 carrot, diced
- 2 cloves garlic, minced
- 1 tbs. flour (optional)
- 40 oz. vegetable stock
- 1 sweet potato, cut into small cubes
- 15 oz. package frozen corn
- Salt and pepper, to taste

1. Heat oil in a large pot and sauté onion, carrot, and garlic over low heat for about 5 minutes until soft
2. Stir in flour and cook for 1 minute
3. Add vegetable stock and stir well
4. Add sweet potato, bring to a boil, then simmer approx. 20 minutes
5. Stir in corn and cook for 5 minutes
6. Remove 2 cups of soup to a food processor or blender and blend until smooth
7. Return to pot, mix thoroughly, season with salt and pepper, and reheat
8. Serve immediately

3 Bean Vegan Bean Chili

Serves approx 6

- 1–2 tbs. olive oil
- 1 medium onion, finely chopped
- 2 bell peppers (red, yellow, or orange), chopped
- 1–2 jalapeño peppers, chopped (depending on desired heat)
- 3 cloves garlic, finely chopped
- 2 tsp ground cumin
- 2 tsp dried oregano
- 2 tsp paprika
- 2 tsp salt
- 28 ounce can diced tomatoes
- 2 cups vegetable broth
- 2 tbs. chili powder
- 15 oz. can kidney beans, drained and rinsed
- 15 oz. can black beans, drained and rinsed
- 15 oz. can pinto beans, drained and rinsed
- 15 oz. can corn
- Cilantro
- Green onion/scallions

1. Heat olive oil in large pot. Add onion, bell peppers, jalapeño peppers, and cook 5 minutes. Add garlic, cumin, oregano, paprika, and salt and cook 1–2 minutes until fragrant.

2. Add tomatoes, broth, and chili powder. Stir in all beans and bring to a boil. Reduce heat to low and simmer for 40 minutes, then stir in corn and cook 5 additional minutes. Top with cilantro and green onions and serve.

Salads

Salads are a staple for a Daniel Fast. As part of the weekly meal plan, it's wise to prepare a large portion of salad at the beginning of the week for an easy lunch or side option. Some tips when creating big batches of salad include:

• Using ingredients that will hold throughout the week without wilting or browning.

• Ensuring all toppings and salad dressings are Daniel Fast approved.

• Creating variety so salad doesn't become unpalatable after a few days, and also to ensure you're consuming a variety of nutrients.

Building a delicious salad

With those challenges in mind, here are some guidelines for creating salad in bulk and some recipes to create variety week to week.

1. Use hearty, base vegetables like kale and cabbage.

2. Add bell peppers, cucumbers, broccoli, carrots, and other vegetables with lower water content.

3. Slice green onions, herbs, and vegetables with higher water content, like tomato, and store separately until ready to toss and eat; this is also a good strategy for lighter, more fragile lettuces like arugula or mixed greens.

4. Add beans and legumes for fiber and protein—black beans, garbanzo beans, and peas are great choices.

5. Add fresh or dried fruit like mandarin oranges, sliced strawberries, apples, or dried cranberries.

6. Add nuts and seeds like pumpkin or sunflower seeds.

Asian Salad

Servings vary
- Mixed green and purple cabbage, shredded
- Carrots, shredded
- Red bell pepper, sliced
- Edamame
- Mandarin oranges
- Cilantro
- Sliced almonds

Recommended Salad Dressing: Garlic Sesame

Mediterranean Salad

Servings vary
- Kale, finely chopped
- Romaine lettuce, shredded
- Cucumber, sliced
- Tomatoes, chopped
- Red onion, thinly sliced
- Chickpeas

- Fresh parsley
- Olives

Recommended Salad Dressing: Fresh Lemon

Southwest Salad

Servings

- Romaine lettuce, shredded
- Carrots, shredded
- Green and purple cabbage, shredded
- Tomatoes, chopped
- Red and yellow bell peppers, thinly sliced
- Corn
- Black beans, drained and rinsed
- Avocado, chopped
- Pumpkin seeds
- Cilantro

Recommended Salad Dressing: Cilantro Lime

Garden Salad

Servings

- Kale and romaine lettuces, shredded
- Broccoli, finely chopped
- Carrots, finely chopped

- Cucumbers, chopped
- Peas
- Green Onions, chopped
- Green apple, finely chopped
- Dried cranberries
- Sunflower seeds

Recommended Salad Dressing: Fresh Lemon

Salad Dressings

Fresh Lemon Salad Dressing

- ½ cup fresh squeezed lemon juice
- 4 tbs. shallot, minced
- 4 tsp Dijon mustard (optional)
- 1 ½ tsp salt
- ½ cup olive oil
- ½ cup avocado oil

1. Blend lemon juice, salad, mustard. and salt in a food processor or with an immersion (handheld) blender. Stream in oils and blend until combined.
2. Store in refrigerator up to one week, shake well or blend before each use.

Garlic Sesame Dressing

- ½ cup olive oil
- 2 garlic cloves, minced
- 2 tbs. fresh ginger, minced
- ½ tsp salt
- 2 tbs. liquid aminos (optional)
- 2 tbs. sesame oil

- 2 tbs. sesame seeds

1. Blend all ingredients until well combined.

2. Store in refrigerator up to 1 week, shaking or stirring vigorously before each use.

Cilantro Lime Salad Dressing

- ½ cup olive oil
- ½ cup fresh squeezed lime juice (about 3–4 limes)
- 3 cloves garlic, minced
- ½ cup fresh cilantro, chopped
- 1 tsp salt

1. Blend all ingredients until well combined.

2. Store in refrigerator up to 1 week, shaking or stirring vigorously before each use.

Whole Grains

Whole grains are a nutritious source of complex carbohydrates, fiber, vitamins, and minerals. Quinoa is also a great plant-based source of protein. The basic preparation method for preparing grains is similar. You can also cook grains in the Instant Pot, a rice cooker, or other kitchen tools following manufacturer instructions.

Some options to eating whole grains include as a side dish, in a whole-grain bowl, added to a salad, or for breakfast.

General tips for cooking whole grains

• Follow package directions for the ideal cooking method. Brands can vary slightly in cooking instructions.

• It's recommended to rinse and sort grains in order to remove excess starch and any impurities.

• Vegetable stock can be used in place of water to add flavor if the grains will be used in savory dishes.

• Grains can be cooked in bulk and stored in the refrigerator for 3–5 days if properly sealed.

• Some grains, especially rice, can dry out when stored. When reheating, add a few tablespoons of water, seal tightly, and heat until very hot to steam and add moisture.

• One serving of grain is ¼ cup dry which yields approximately ½ cup cooked.

The recipes below will cook four servings. A serving of cooked grains is half a cup. Adjust ratios to increase or decrease portion sizes. In batch cooking, four cups of cooked grain is a good starting point if you're cooking for multiple meals.

Barley

Serves 4
- 1 cup barley
- 2 ½ cup water or broth

1.Combine barley and water or broth in a saucepan. Bring to boil over high heat, then reduce heat to low and cover.
2.Cook for 10 minutes.
3.Remove from heat and let stand for 5 minutes, then fluff with a fork.

Bulgur

Serves 4
- 1 cup bulgur
- 2 cups water or broth

1. Combine bulgur and water or broth in a medium saucepan. Bring to boil over high heat, then reduce heat to low and cover.
2. Cook for 10 minutes.
3. Remove from heat and let stand for 5 minutes, then fluff with a fork.

Farro

Serves 4

- 1 cup farro, rinsed and sorted
- 1 tsp salt
- 6 cups water or broth

1. Bring a pot of water to a boil and add salt.
2. Add farro and simmer for about 20 minutes or until al dente like pasta, tasting to test doneness.
3. Remove from heat and drain excess water.
4. Let stand for 5 minutes, then fluff with a fork.

Quinoa

Serves 4

- 1 cup quinoa, rinsed and sorted
- 2 cups water or broth
- 1 tsp salt (optional)

1. Combine water and quinoa in a medium saucepan and bring to a boil. Add salt if desired.
2. Cover the pan with a tight-fitting lid and simmer on low heat for 15–20 minutes, until liquid is absorbed.
3. Remove from heat and let stand for 5 minutes, then fluff with a fork.

Brown rice

Serves 4

- 1 cup brown rice
- 2 ½ cups water or broth
- ½ tsp salt (optional)

1. Combine water, rice, and salt in a medium saucepan and bring to a boil.
2. Stir and cover with a tight-fitting lid. Reduce heat and simmer on low for 40–45 minutes, until liquid is absorbed.
3. Remove from heat and let stand for 10 minutes, then fluff with a fork.

Notes: Cook time and ratios may vary depending on the type of rice used: long grain, short grain, basmati, etc.

Other whole-grain options

The five types of grain listed above are typically easy to find in a major grocery store. However, there are additional whole grains with tremendous nutritional value and taste. One of the great aspects of cooking with whole grains is their versatility. You can easily substitute either rice or quinoa in a bowl, or top a salad with either barley or bulgur

You can also experiment with some other whole grains such as:

- Amaranth
- Buckwheat
- Millet
- Wheat berries or cracked wheat

Whole Grain Stir-frys

You're probably familiar with stir-frys. This is an easy go-to meal for a Daniel Fast; simply add veggies and toppings to rice or another grain of choice. The tricky part of preparing a stir-fry during a Daniel Fast is adjusting the sauces you may typically enjoy in an unrestricted diet.

If you follow a strict interpretation of the Daniel fast, you can steam vegetables and serve them on rice. If you stir-fry, you'll have to use some form of oil like olive or sesame oil to prevent sticking. Any of the following ingredients can be used to create a stir-fry bowl.

Vegetables for Stir-fry

- Broccoli
- Carrots
- Mushrooms (try shiitake or stir-fry blend)
- Bok Choy
- Chinese/Napa cabbage
- Snow peas/peas
- Corn
- Bell Peppers
- Green Beans
- Garlic
- Onions

Stir-fry Toppings

- Water chestnuts
- Sesame seeds
- Sliced almonds
- Cashews
- Peanuts
- Cilantro
- Sesame oil
- Bragg's (or other brand) liquid aminos
- Coconut milk
- Ginger
- Fresh cilantro
- Fresh lime

Whole Grain Bowls

A whole grain bowl "recipe" can follow a very simple formula. Really, it's about layering a variety of ingredients for textures and flavors that pair well together. Whole grain bowls are one of my absolute favorite meals because they provide a complete set of nutrients from whole grains, vegetables, and nuts or seeds.

Basic Whole-Grain Bowl Recipe

Per serving
- ½ cup cooked whole grains (quinoa, rice, farro, etc.)
- 1–2 cups cooked or raw vegetables
- 1/2 cup fresh fruit or ¼ cup dried fruit (optional)
- 1–2 tbs. seeds or nuts
- 1 tbs. fresh herbs

Layer all ingredients and enjoy.

Southwest Whole Grain Bowl

Serves 2
- 1 cup quinoa, cooked
- ¼ cup black beans
- ¼ cup corn, fresh or frozen
- 1 cup raw bell peppers and onions, sliced

- 1 cup romaine lettuce, thinly sliced
- ½ cup fresh tomatoes, chopped
- ½ avocado, sliced
- 2 tbs. pumpkin seeds
- 2 tbs. fresh cilantro
- Fresh lime
- Olive oil

1. Divide quinoa between two bowls.

2. Drain excess liquid from canned or previously cooked black beans. Thaw corn if using frozen. Divide beans and corn between two bowls.

3. Sauté bell peppers and onions 4–5 minutes in a skillet with a small amount of olive oil, then add to the bowls.

4. Top with fresh lettuce, tomatoes, avocado, and pumpkin seeds.

5. Garnish with fresh lime and cilantro.

Mediterranean Farro Whole-Grain Bowl

Serves 2

- 1 cup farro, cooked
- ½ zucchini, sliced in half then cut into even sticks
- 1 red bell pepper, sliced into strips
- ½ cup chickpeas, drained and rinsed
- 1 cup fresh spinach

- ½ cup fresh tomatoes, chopped
- ¼ cup Kalamata olives, pitted
- 2 tbs. fresh parsley
- Fresh lemon
- Olive oil

1. Preheat oven to 400 degrees.

2. Drizzle zucchini and bell pepper with olive oil and place on a baking sheet. Roast for 20 minutes or until done. Remove from oven and cool slightly.

3. Divide farro, zucchini, peppers, and all other ingredients between two bowls.

4. Finish with fresh parsley and lemon.

Roasted Veggie and Bulgur Whole-Grain Bowl

Serves 2

- 1 cup bulgur, cooked
- 1 small sweet potato, peeled and chopped into uniform chunks
- 1 cup Brussels sprouts, trimmed and cut in half
- 1 cup cauliflower florets, cut into uniform pieces
- 1 cup mixed greens (spring mix or kale)
- ¼ red onion, sliced
- 2 tbs. fresh Italian parsley
- Olive oil

1. Preheat oven to 400 degrees.

2. Drizzle sweet potato, Brussels sprouts, and cauliflower with olive oil and place on a baking sheet. Roast for 30–40 minutes or until done, stirring halfway through cook time. Remove from oven and cool slightly.

3. Divide bulgur and roasted veggies between bowls.

4. Top with greens, onion, and fresh parsley.

Hearty Whole-Grain Salads

Bulgur Salad with Carrots and Cilantro

Serves 4-6

- 1 ½ cups dry bulgur
- 1 cup water or broth
- 2 lemons, juiced
- ¼ cup olive oil
- ½ tsp ground cumin
- ¼ tsp garlic powder
- ¾ tsp salt
- 2 cups carrots, shredded
- 2 green onions, sliced
- ½ cup sliced almonds
- ¼ cup fresh cilantro, chopped

1. Combine bulgur, water, juice of 1 lemon, and ¼ tsp salt. Cover and allow to sit at room temperature for approximately 1.5 hours until softened, drain any remaining liquid.

2. Combine 2 tbs. lemon juice, olive oil, cumin, garlic powder, and ½ tsp salt and whisk until combined.

3. Lightly toast almonds in a skillet on medium-low heat.

4. Add carrots to bulgur. Add olive oil mixture, almonds, green onions, and cilantro and toss until combined.

Pearl Couscous with Roasted Tomatoes

Serves 4

- 2 cups cherry tomatoes
- 4–5 cloves garlic, peeled
- 2 tbs. olive oil
- 1 cup couscous
- 1 1/2 cups broth or water
- 1 cup loosely packed spinach, lightly chopped
- ½ lemon
- ¼ cup pine nuts
- Fresh parsley for garnish
- Salt and pepper to taste

1. Preheat oven to 425 degrees. Toss tomatoes and garlic with 1 tbs. olive oil and place in an ovenproof dish. Roast 7–10 minutes until soft and skins have burst. Remove and allow to cool slightly.

2. Cook the pearl couscous according to package instructions. Fluff with a fork.

3. Combine couscous with tomatoes, garlic, spinach, and remaining oil. Season with salt and pepper, garnish with pine nuts, parsley, and a squeeze of lemon.

Chickpea and Quinoa Salad

Serves 4

- 1 cup dry quinoa
- 15 oz. can chickpeas, drained and rinsed
- ⅔ cup chickpea flour
- 2 tsp cumin
- 1 tsp paprika
- 3 tbs. avocado or olive oil
- ½ red bell pepper, chopped
- 3 green onions, thinly sliced
- 2 tbs. fresh lemon juice
- Salt and pepper to taste

1. Cook quinoa according to package directions. Fluff with a fork and transfer to a large bowl.

2. Whisk 2 tbs. olive oil and lemon juice together in a small bowl.

3. Sift chickpea flour, cumin, and paprika. Pat chickpeas dry and roll them in flour mixture. Shake off excess flour. Heat 1 tbs. olive oil in a skillet over medium heat and cook flour-coated chickpeas in batches for 3–4 minutes or until brown.

4. Stir chickpeas into quinoa along with red bell peppers. Top with green onions and lemon oil dressing. Add salt and pepper to taste.

Veggie Entrees

Cashew Chickpea Curry

Serves 4

- 1 cup brown rice, cooked
- 1 cup potatoes, diced
- 3 tbs. olive oil or coconut oil
- ¼ cup onion, chopped
- 2 garlic cloves, minced
- 1–2 tbs. fresh ginger, peeled and finely chopped
- 1 tsp cumin
- 1 tsp chili powder
- ½ tsp turmeric
- ½ cup vegan stock
- 15 oz. can of chickpeas, drained and rinsed
- 1 cup cashew nuts (halves or pieces)
- 15 oz. can coconut milk
- Fresh cilantro and green onion for garnish

1. Fill a saucepan halfway with water and heat to boiling. Add diced potatoes and cook for 10–15 minutes, until tender when pierced with a fork.

2. Heat 1 tbs. oil over medium heat and sauté onion, garlic, ginger, and spices for 5 minutes until onion is soft.

3. Stir in cooked potatoes, drained chickpeas, and cashew nuts and cook for 2–3 more minutes.

4. Stir in vegetable stock and coconut milk. Reduce heat to low and cook for approximately 15 minutes, until creamy.

5. Garnish with cilantro and green onion and serve over brown rice.

Portabella Mushroom Caps with Veggies

Serves 4

- 4 large Portabella mushroom caps
- 2 tbs. olive oil
- ½ cup yellow onion, diced
- 1 small–medium zucchini, diced
- ½ cup bell pepper, diced (any color)
- 3 sun-dried tomatoes, chopped
- 2 cloves garlic, minced
- ½ tsp dried oregano
- ½ tsp salt
- 2 cups fresh spinach

1. Preheat oven to 375 degrees. Line a baking sheet with parchment paper or foil.

2. Clean mushrooms, scoop out gills, and remove stump. Rub outside of mushroom with olive oil and place on baking sheet top down, stalk side up.

3. Heat remaining olive oil in a large skillet. Add onion and cook 3–4 minutes. Add zucchini and cook an additional 3–4 minutes. Add bell pepper, tomatoes, oregano, salt, and garlic and continue to cook. Add spinach and stir until wilted.

4. Remove from heat. Stir all ingredients and spoon into mushroom caps.

5. Bake approximately 30 minutes, until vegetables are tender and slightly browned. Remove from oven and allow to cool 5 minutes before serving.

Southwest Corn and Black Bean Sweet Potatoes

6 servings
- 3 medium sweet potatoes
- 1 cup black beans, drained and rinsed
- ½ cup frozen corn, thawed
- ¼ cup onion, diced
- ½ cup red pepper, diced
- 1 cup spinach, chopped
- 2 tsp fresh jalapeño pepper, finely diced
- ½ tsp chili powder
- ¼ tsp cumin
- ¼ tsp cinnamon
- ¼ tsp paprika
- ½ tsp olive oil

Avocado drizzle:

- 1 large avocado
- ¼ cup lemon juice
- ¼ cup water

1. Preheat oven to 350F

2. Prick sweet potatoes with a fork and bake for about 1 hour or until tender. Remove sweet potatoes from oven and allow to cool for 5–10 minutes.

3. Slice sweet potatoes in half and scoop out the flesh, leaving a thin layer of potato inside the skin so they maintain their shape and can hold the filling. Place skins back onto the tray and spray lightly with olive oil. Return to oven and bake for 6–8 minutes, allowing the skins to get crispy.

4. Mash the scooped out sweet potato. Add the black beans, frozen corn, red peppers, onion, jalapeño pepper, and spices. Stir until well combined.

5. Remove skins from the oven and fill each skin with the sweet potato and bean mixture.

6. Bake again for 20–25 minutes, or until heated through.

Avocado drizzle

Place all ingredients for avocado drizzle into a blender or food processor and blend until smooth, then drizzle over sweet potato halves.

Mediterranean Stuffed Bell Peppers

Serves 4

- 4 bell peppers
- 2 ½ cups quinoa, cooked
- ½ cup tomato, diced
- ¼ cup red onion, finely chopped
- ½ tsp Italian seasoning
- Salt and pepper
- ¼ cup cucumber, chopped
- ¼ cup fresh parsley, chopped
- 2 tbs. kalamata olives

1. Preheat oven to 350 degrees and cook quinoa according to package instructions then allow to cool slightly.
2. Cut tops off bell peppers and clean out seeds and ribs.
3. Mix cooked quinoa, tomato, red onion, Italian seasoning, salt, and pepper until combined.
4. Fill bell peppers leaving about one inch of space at the top.
5. Bake filled peppers at 350 degrees for about 30 minutes.
6. Mix cucumber, olives, and fresh parsley and spoon mixture onto tops of cooked bell peppers.
7. Finish with a squeeze of fresh lemon and enjoy immediately.

Easy Roasted Vegetable Recipe

Serves 6–8

- 1 red onion, quartered
- ½ butternut squash, cubed
- 2 medium sweet potatoes, cubed
- 8 oz. fingerling potatoes
- 8 oz. carrots, sliced
- 16 oz. Brussels sprouts, halved
- 2 red bell peppers, sliced
- ¼ cup olive oil
- ½ tsp garlic powder
- ½ tsp onion powder
- 1 tsp salt
- ½ tsp pepper
- ¼ cup fresh parsley (optional garnish)

1. Preheat oven to 400 degrees.
2. Wash and cut vegetables, trying to keep them uniform in size for more even cooking.
3. Whisk together oil, garlic powder, onion powder, salt, and pepper and toss vegetables to coat.
4. Spread evenly on two shallow pans or baking sheets and cook 35–45 minutes, stirring every 10 minutes and rotating pans halfway through cook time.

5. Allow vegetables to cool slightly, garnish with fresh parsley, additional salt and pepper to taste, and serve.

Notes: There are a variety of vegetables good for roasting, and you can alter the actual vegetables used in the medley to suit your taste.

Vegetable Paella

Serves 6

- 4 oz. artichokes in water, drained and sliced lengthwise
- 2 red bell peppers, sliced
- 4 whole garlic cloves, peeled
- ¼ cup olive oil
- 2 tbs. lemon juice
- 2 tbs. fresh Italian parsley
- ½ onion, chopped
- ½ tsp paprika
- 14.5oz can diced tomatoes, drained and chopped
- 2 cups arborio or short grain rice
- 3 cups vegetable broth
- ½ tsp saffron (optional)
- 1 tsp salt
- ½ cup kalamata olives, halved or sliced
- ½ cup peas, thawed

1. Preheat oven to 450 degrees.

2. Line a baking sheet with foil or silicone mat. Toss artichokes, bell peppers, and whole garlic cloves with 2 tbs. olive oil and spread in pan. Roast for 20–25 minutes or until vegetables are browned. Reduce oven temperature to 350 degrees.

3. Whisk olive oil, lemon juice, parsley, and minced roasted garlic in a bowl until combined. Toss with roasted vegetables.

4. Heat 1 tbs. olive oil in a Dutch oven and sauté onion until softened. Stir in paprika and diced tomatoes. Cook about 3–4 minutes, stirring frequently, then add rice and stir to combine. Add broth, saffron, and 1 tsp salt. Bring to a boil over medium-high heat. Cover and transfer to the oven to bake for 25–35 minutes, until rice is cooked.

5. Remove rice, then add roasted vegetables, olives, and peas, cover, and allow to sit for 5–10 minutes. Garnish with lemon juice, fresh parsley, and salt and pepper to taste.

Spaghetti Squash with Tomato Sauce

Serves 4–6
- 1 medium-large spaghetti squash
- 1 tbs. olive oil
- ½ medium onion, chopped
- 2 tbs. fresh parsley, chopped
- 1–2 cloves garlic, minced
- ½ tsp dried basil or 2 tbs. fresh basil, chopped

- 28 oz. can diced tomatoes, undrained
- 2 tbs. tomato paste
- Salt and pepper

1. Microwave spaghetti squash for a few minutes to soften skin, then cut in half lengthwise and scoop out seeds.
2. Place squash cut side down in a large baking dish, add ¼ to ½ cup water.
3. Bake approximately 30 minutes, until squash is tender.
4. Take a fork and gently rake the inside of the squash to pull out spaghetti-like strands.

Sauce
1. Heat olive oil and sauté onion for 4–5 minutes. Add parsley, garlic, and basil and sauté 1–2 minutes more.
2. Add in tomatoes and tomato paste. Heat to boiling, then reduce heat to low and simmer about 15 minutes. Add salt and pepper to taste.

Snack Options

When fasting, you may decide to not only limit what types of food you eat but also how often you are eating. For example, you may follow the Daniel Fast in your food choices, but also eat just one or two solid meals a day and consume liquids for the remaining part of the day. If that's the case, you may skip over this snacking section entirely.

If you have health restrictions, and that's part of the reason you chose a Daniel fast, it may be beneficial or recommended that you eat small meals every 3–4 hours for sustained energy.

There is not necessarily a delineation between what constitutes a snack versus a meal for the Daniel Fast meal plan, but here are some foods to keep in mind when you're looking for snack options.

Sample of Daniel Fast Snacks

- Raw vegetables
- Whole fruits
- Mixed berries
- Fruit salad
- Dried fruit
- Raw, unsalted nuts or seeds—almonds, cashews, pumpkin seeds
- Celery with peanut butter or almond butter
- Apples with peanut butter or almond butter
- Smoothies
- Fresh juices (blended)
- ½ fresh avocado
- Cucumber and tomato salad

Roasted Chickpeas

- 15 oz. can of garbanzo beans/chickpeas
- 2 tbs. olive oil
- 1 tsp salt
- 1 tsp garlic powder (optional)

1. Preheat oven to 450 degrees.

2. Drain and rinse chickpeas, pat dry. Toss with olive oil, salt, and garlic powder.

3. Spread evenly in pan and roast for 30–40 minutes, stirring halfway through cook time.

Simple Guacamole

- ½ avocado
- ½ tsp salt
- 1 tbs. lime juice
- 2 tbs. tomato and onion, diced
- 1 tbs. fresh cilantro

Mash avocado and mix all ingredients. Serve with vegetables.

Homemade Hummus

- 2 tbs. fresh lemon juice
- 2 tbs. tahini
- 15 oz. can chickpeas, rinsed
- 1–2 cloves garlic, peeled and minced
- ¼ cup olive oil plus 2 tbs. for serving
- 1 tsp ground cumin
- 1 tsp kosher salt
- Water as needed
- ½ tsp paprika

Optional toppings: roasted red peppers, chopped olives, or pine nuts.

1. Combine tahini and lemon juice in food processor or blender and process for 45-60 seconds.

2. Add chickpeas, garlic, ¼ cup olive oil, cumin and salt and process until smooth. Add cold water 1 tbs. at a time until desired consistency is reached.

3. Drizzle with 2 tbs. olive oil, sprinkle with paprika and add optional toppings if desired.

APPENDIX

Appendix 1

Biblical References to Fasting and Abstaining from Food

Exodus 34:28	Moses fasting on Mt Sinai for forty days and forty nights
Leviticus 16:29,31	Day of Atonement
Leviticus 23:14	Not eating until the sheaf of wave offering is brought in
Numbers 6:3-4	Food and drink to abstain from as a Nazirite
Deuteronomy 9:9, 18	References to the two times Moses fasted for 40 days and 40 nights
Judges 20:26	Sons of Israel fasting in their battle against the tribe of Benjamin
1 Samuel 1:7-8	Hannah in prayer and distress over having a child
1 Samuel 7:5	Sons of Israel fasting in repentance under Samuel at Mizpah
1 Samuel 20:34	Jonathan did not eat in worry for David

1 Samuel 31:13 &	
1 Chronicles 10:12	Saul's men fasted seven days after the death of Saul and his sons
2 Samuel 1:12	David and his men fasted and mourned in response to Saul's death
2 Samuel 3:35	David fasting and mourning in response to Abner's death
2 Samuel 12:16,2	David fasting for his child by Bathsheba that had become sick
1 Kings 13:8-9	Man of God who warned King Jeroboam at Bethel
1 Kings 17:4-6	Elijah fed bread and meat by ravens twice a day
1 Kings 19:8	Elijah traveling forty days and nights to Mt. Horeb
1 Kings 21:4-5	King Ahab refusing to eat after Naboth's refusal
1 Kings 21:9,12	Fast proclaimed by Jezebel to trap Naboth
1 Kings 21:27-29	King Ahab after encounter with Elijah
2 Chronicles 20:3-4	Fast proclaimed by King Jehoshaphat before battle
Ezra 8:21-23	Fast proclaimed by Ezra at river of Ahava in humility, for safe passage
Ezra 10:6	Ezra mourning over the unfaithfulness of the exiles
Nehemiah 1:4	Nehemiah fasting and mourning over the state of Jerusalem
Nehemiah 9:1	Sons of Israel assembled in fasting and confession of sins
Esther 4:3	Jews fasting and mourning because of the king's decree incited by Haman

Esther 4:16	Esther proclaims a three day fast for the Jews before going to the king
Esther 9:31	Instructions for fasting during Purim
Psalms 35:13	David fasting and praying for the sick
Psalms 69:10	Fasting and chastening the soul
Psalms 109:24	Fasting making one weak
Isaiah 58	The fast acceptable to the Lord
Jeremiah 14:12	An unacceptable fast
Jeremiah 36:6	Day of fasting (Day of Atonement)
Daniel 1:1-12-17	Daniel refusing to consume meat and wine
Daniel 6:18	Darius while Daniel was in the lion's den
Daniel 9:3	Daniel praying and repenting for Jerusalem
Daniel 10:2-3	Daniel's 21 day partial fast
Joel 1:14, 2:15	Call to consecrate a fast
Joel 2:12	Fast and return to God with the whole heart
Jonah 3:5-10	A fast of repentance for the people of Nineveh
Zechariah 7:5-6	Fasting in fifth and seventh months
Zechariah 8:19	Fasts of the fourth, fifth, seventh and tenth months
Matt 4:2, Luke 4:2	Jesus fasting forty days in the wilderness
Matthew 6:16-18	Jesus's instructions to his disciples on how to fast
Matt 9:14-15, Mark 2:18-20, Luke 5:33-35	Fasting by John's disciples and the Pharisees; fasting when the bridegroom is gone

Matt 17:21,	
Mark 9:29*	This kind goes out by prayer and fasting
	*King James Version
Luke 2:37	Anna worshiping in the temple
Luke 18:11-12	Fasting by the boastful Pharisee
Acts 9:9, 19	Saul after encountering Christ on road to Damascus
Acts 13:2-3	Prophets and teachers ministering to the Lord in church at Antioch
Acts 14:23	Prayer and fasting when anointing elders in the church
Acts 27:9	Reference to Day of Atonement
Romans 14:13-21	Not causing a stumbling block
1 Corinthians 8:13	Not causing a brother to stumble

Appendix 2

Ingredients to Avoid on the Daniel Fast

Ingredient lists can be tricky to decipher when they're filled with unrecognizable and unpronounceable words. As a general rule, if it's not a whole, plant-based ingredient, don't eat it. As you look at nutrition labels on foods you are purchasing, be sure to exclude any of the following ingredients.

Egg-based Ingredients
- Albumin
- Cholesterol free egg substitute (e.g. Eggbeaters®)
- Dried egg solids, dried egg
- Egg, egg white, egg yolk
- Egg wash eggnog
- Globulin
- Mayonnaise

- Meringue, meringue powder
- Ovalbumin

Milk-based Ingredients

- Casein and Caseinates
- Creams
- Curds
- Custard
- Ghee
- Hydrolysates
- Lactalbumin, lavatase
- Nougat
- Whey
- Yogurt

Sweeteners

- Anything containing the word "sugar" or "syrup"
- Aspartame
- Sucrose
- High-fructose corn syrup
- Barley malt
- Dextrose, dextrin
- Erythritol
- Galactose
- Glucose, glucose solids

- Maltodextrin, maltose
- Saccharin
- Stevia
- Sucralose (Splenda)
- Xylitol

Foods That Often Contain Yeast

- Bread and baked goods
- Alcohol or cider (any ingredient with "alcohol" listed)
- Premade stocks, soups, and gravies
- Vinegar or foods that have been pickled, preserved with vinegar such as sauerkraut
- Soy sauce, miso, tamari
- Tofu

Appendix 3

Daniel Fast Foods FAQ

"Can I eat this?" Below are some commonly asked questions about food items for a Daniel Fast. The answers usually depend on which filter you have chosen. Most of the time, the question can be answered with this question: Are you simply abstaining from animal products, or are you limiting your fast to only eating plant-based foods in their whole, natural form?

Below is additional information to consider for some food items you might be unsure of including. Before you fast, decide how you will handle these items and others that come to mind.

Agave, honey, maple syrup, and monk fruit: Agave, monk fruit, and maple syrup (not artificially flavored, but true maple syrup) are plant-based sweeteners that come from nature, but technically, so is white cane sugar. Honey is produced by bees, so could be considered an animal product. Most fasts exclude all added sweeteners, whether natural or artificial.

Artificial sweeteners (equal, aspartame, Splenda, Stevia, etc): My personal opinion is none of these should be included. Although some options, like Stevia, may be better for you than actual aspartame, I recommend no sweeteners out of colored packets in general. Aside from fasting, there is enough evidence that artificial sweeteners have negative, long-term health consequences that I do not recommend them at all.

Flat and pita bread: Bread was a staple of the daily diet in biblical times, and there were variations of both leavened (containing yeast) and unleavened (no yeast) bread. While most people would agree that any products containing yeast should not be eaten on a Daniel Fast, unleavened bread, such as pita bread or flatbreads, might be eaten on a Daniel Fast depending on the parameters you have chosen.

Ezekiel brand bread products: Although based on the Bible verse Ezekiel 4:9, these products contain other ingredients beyond pure grains, including yeast. So for reasons mentioned above, the Ezekiel brand bread products containing yeast would not be included on a Daniel plan.

Flour alternatives (almond, coconut, chickpea, oat, etc.): All of these flours can be eaten on a Daniel Fast. Traditional 100 percent whole wheat flour can technically be used since wheat is a plant, although it can be beneficial to avoid gluten while fasting.

Milk/Yogurt substitutes (almond, cashew, coconut, oat, etc): The nutritional value of milk substitutes has been a subject of debate.

One of the chief issues is to ensure that although they are called "milk," these products are not a direct substitution for cow's milk since they have a different nutritional composition in terms of protein, fat, vitamins, and calcium.

The other potential issue with milk substitutes is the added ingredients and preservatives in processing. Look carefully at ingredient lists to find the brands with the least number of additives, and if you're following a more limited version of the Daniel Fast, these would be foods to avoid.

Nut butters (almond, cashew, sunflower, or peanut butter): Nut butters vary in level of processing. Some health food stores and grocery stores have machines that allow you to grind your own nuts to provide a nut butter in pure form. There are also natural mainstream brands ready for purchase. If avoiding processed foods, than you would abstain from these.

Soy products: Soy products, including soy milk, soybeans, edamame, tofu, and tempeh, have claimed health benefits and also been accused of health risks. Potential risks of soy include the negative impact of phytoestrogens on hormones and thyroid function. Another source of debate is that most soy products in the US are genetically modified. The FDA estimates that 93 percent of soybeans planted are genetically engineered (https://www.fda.gov/food/food-new-plant-varieties/consumer-info-about-food-genetically-engineered-plants).

Triscuits or unleavened crackers: Triscuits do not contain yeast so some people eat them on a Daniel Fast. However, they are processed, so if you're eating only whole, non-processed foods then skip these.

Vegan protein powder: Although vegan protein powders by definition contain no animal products, there may still be a number of preservatives. If you are trying to eat a purely unprocessed, whole-food diet, then do not include these.

Vegetable patties (soy, black bean): Depending on the approach you're taking, you can find alternative meat products that are purely vegetable-based, but most frozen foods contain a large number of preservatives and often soy, salt, and other additives. You can also make veggie patties at home and control the ingredients you're including.

Vinegar: Vinegar is a solution of an acid derived from alcohol. After alcohol is fermented, it produces a solution containing acetic acid which is the component that gives vinegar its sour, acidic flavor. Even though vinegar contains a trace, if any, amount of actual alcohol, it could contain yeast, although distilled vinegar will not contain yeast in most cases.

Although it is not technically alcoholic, some choose to abstain from anything fermented or used as a flavoring agent while on a Daniel Fast. Balsamic vinegar is a type of vinegar derived from grapes rather than alcohol but may contain sugar and thickening agents.

Other Questions

Should everything I eat be organic? To advertise as organic, produce needs to meet certain qualifications for pesticide use and agricultural methods while being grown and processed. Although it's better to avoid these chemicals and pesticides and eat organic, it can also be more expensive and is not required for a Daniel Fast.

What if I mess up and eat something I wasn't supposed to? We are human, and you may slip up at a certain point on your fast because you're mentally frustrated, physically exhausted, socially pressured, or for other reasons. There's no need to beat yourself up, nor should you completely abandon your fasting effort. As soon as you can (your next meal), get back on track. Remember progress, not perfection.

Acknowledgements

First and foremost, thanks to my husband and children who were extremely patient as I poured hours upon hours into this book. I am so grateful for your encouragement and support.

My deepest gratitude to the entire Self-Publishing School community, Chandler Bolt, and my coach Ellaine Ursuy. The lessons and coaching, along with the support and accountability of the tribe, are valuable beyond measure.

I had an incredible team assist me with production of this book. I could not ask for more excellent professionals to work with. Katie Chambers (Beacon Point LLC) took this book to another level in the editing process. Susan Michaud (The Sage Proofreader) was meticulous, prompt, and delightful to work with. Finally, Alejandro Martin provided above and beyond service in formatting this book.

I also have to thank my friend Danielle Wingate and the Catalyst Women community. That retreat really was a turning point in my life! I am so thankful for the support, encouragement, and prayers when I needed them most throughout the process of writing this book.

Finally, I thank God for all of it. For giving me the opportunity to write this book and carry this message. For inspiring the original content, giving me the nudge to step forward and actually write this book, and carrying me through every step of the way.

About the Author

Stephanie Hodges has pursued information concerning exercise, healthy eating, and holistic health and wellness from the time she was a teenager. In college, she obtained certifications as a group fitness instructor and personal trainer and specialty certifications in spinning, yoga, Pilates, and more. After earning her master's in Nutrition and Exercise Science, she worked in university campus recreation programs, small private gyms, large franchise gyms, and in the corporate wellness setting. In these roles, she has worked with clients from a variety of backgrounds, ranging in age from teenagers to those in their sixties.

After over fifteen years serving in ministry in a variety of capacities, including seven years in full-time ministry on staff at a large church, she has realized the critical importance of integrating the health of body, soul, and spirit. Just as she has helped her three kids and countless students and church members build a healthy life one choice and one small step at a time, she can help you too. Her passion is helping others to pursue wellness by making healthy choices daily. Stephanie lives just north of Austin, Texas with her husband and three children.

Book Resources

Visit www.danielfastjourney.com/bookresources to view the resources and handouts mentioned in this book. These resources include:

- Daniel Fast Planning & Reflection Journal
- Daily Journal Sheet
- Biblical References to Fasting and Abstaining from Food
- Daniel Fast Journey Food Lists
- Daniel Fast Journey Meal Template
- Daniel Fast Journey 21 Day Meal Plan

Could you take a second to leave a review on Amazon?

I am grateful and honored that you took the time to read this book, and I sincerely hope you found it helpful. It would be unbelievably helpful for me and other readers if you would leave an honest review on Amazon. Thank you!

Endnotes

I "Tsuwm—Strong's Hebrew Lexicon (KJV)," Blue Letter Bible, accessed November 15, 2019, https://www.blueletterbible.org/lang/lexicon/lexicon.cfm?Strongs=H6684&t=KJV.

II "Nesteuo—Alpha Strong's Greek Lexicon (KJV)," Blue Letter Bible, accessed August 30, 2020.https://www.blueletterbible.org/lang/lexicon/lexicon.cfm?Strongs=G3522&t=NASB.

III Dictionary.com, s.v. "journey," accessed November 15, 2019, https://www.dictionary.com/browse/journey?s=t.

IV Merriam-Webster, s.v. "holistic," accessed November 16, 2019, https://www.merriam-webster.com/dictionary/holistic.

V "1 Thessalonians 5:23:: New American Standard Bible," Blue Letter Bible, accessed October 10, 2020, https://www.blueletterbible.org/nasb/1th/5/23/t_conc_1116023.

VI Claire E. Berryman, Harris R. Lieberman, Victor L. Fulgoni 3rd, et al, "Protein intake trends and conformity with the Dietary Reference Intakes in the United States: analysis of the National Health and Nutrition Examination Survey," Am J Clin Nutr 108, no. 2 (August 2018): 405–413, https://pubmed.ncbi.nlm.nih.gov/29931213/.

VII Daniel Pendick, "How much protein do you need every day?" Harvard Health Publishing, posted June 18, 2015, https://www.health.harvard.edu/blog/how-much-protein-do-you-need-every-day-201506188096.

VIII "Adult Obesity Causes & Consequences," Center for Disease Control and Prevention, last updated September 17, 2020, https://www.cdc.gov/obesity/adult/causes.html.

IX Colin T Campbell, The China Study: Startling Implications for Diet Weight Loss and Long-Term Health (repr., Dallas, Texas: Benbella Books, 2006).

X Forks Over Knives. Directed and Written by by Lee Fulkerson, 2011.

XI Dan Buettner, 2015. The Blue Zones Solution (repr., Washington D.C.: National Geographic Society, 2017).

XII Valter Longo, The Longevity Diet (Penguin Random House, 2018).

XIII "Gymnazo—Alpha Strong's Greek Lexicon (KJV)," Blue Letter Bible, accessed August 15, 2020, https://www.blueletterbible.org/lang/lexicon/lexicon.cfm?Strongs=G1128&t=NASB.

XIV "Temptation of Jesus—Bible Story," Bible Study Tools, accessed August 19, 2019, https://www.biblestudytools.com/bible-stories/temptation-of-jesus-bible-story.html.

XV See Mark 2:18–20, Matthew 9:14–17, and Luke 5:33–38

XVI Online Etymology Dictionary, s.v. "discipline," accessed August 17, 2020, https://www.etymonline.com/word/discipline.

XVII Jon Simpson, "Finding Brand Success in the Digital World," Forbes, August 25,2017, https://www.forbes.com/sites/forbesagencycouncil/2017/08/25/finding-brand-success-in-the-digital-world/?sh=7d0d9021626e.

XVIII "Shachah—Strong's Hebrew Lexicon (NASB)," Blue Letter Bible, accessed August 17, 2020, https://www.blueletterbible.org/lang/lexicon/lexicon.cfm?Strongs=H7812&t=NASB.

XIX Wikipedia, s.v. "Meditation," accessed May 15, 2020, https://en.wikipedia.org/wiki/Meditation.

XX "Stress Facts and Tips," American Psychological Association, accessed August 27, 2020, https://www.apa.org/topics/stress/index.html.

XXI Madhav Goyal, "Meditation programs for psychological stress and well-being: a systematic
review and meta-analysis," JAMA Internal Medicine 174 no. 3 (2014): 357–68.

XXII "Hagah—Strong's Hebrew Lexicon (NASB)," Blue Letter Bible, accessed May 15, 2020,

https://www.blueletterbible.org/lang/lexicon/lexicon.
cfm?Strongs=H1897&t=NASB.

XXIII Teruhisa Komori, "The relaxation effect of prolonged expiratory breathing,"
Mental Illness 10 no. 1 (2018):6–7, accessed November 8, 2020, https://
www.ncbi.nlm.nih.gov/pmc/articles/PMC6037091/.

XXIV Arianna Huffington, The Sleep Revolution: Transforming Your Life, One
Night at a Time (New York: Harmony Books).

XXV Eric Suni, "Healthy Sleep Tips," Sleep Foundation, last updated July 30,
2020, https://www.sleepfoundation.org/articles/healthy-sleep-tips.

XXVI Miriam F. Vamosh, Food at the Time of the Bible (Abingdon Press, 2004).

XXVII Cheryl D. Fryar et. al, "Fast Food Consumption Among Adults in the United States, 2013–2016," National Center for Health Statistics, October 2018,
https://www.cdc.gov/nchs/products/databirefts/db322.htm.

XXVIII "Only 1 in 10 Adults Get Enough Fruits or Vegetables," CDC News-
room, November 16, 2017, https://www.cdc.gov/media/releases/2017/
p1116-fruit-vegetable-consumption.html.

XXIX "Zeroa—Strong's Hebrew Lexicon (KJV)," Blue Letter Bible, accessed November 29, 2019,

https://www.blueletterbible.org/lang/lexicon/lexicon.

cfm?Strongs=H2235&t=KJV.

XXX Miriam F. Vamosh, Food at the Time of the Bible (Abingdon Press, 2004).

XXXI Ibid.

XXXII "Peripateo—Strong's Greek Lexicon (NASB)," Blue Letter Bible, accessed August 12, 2020, https://www.blueletterbible.org/lang/lexicon/lexicon.

cfm?Strongs=G4043&t=NASB.

Printed in Great Britain
by Amazon